THE DESIGN AND DEVELOPMENT OF THE
HAWKER HUNTER

THE DESIGN AND DEVELOPMENT OF THE
HAWKER HUNTER
THE CREATION OF BRITAIN'S ICONIC JET FIGHTER

TONY BUTTLER

The
History
Press

To Peter Green, a master collector of aircraft photographs and documents since the 1940s. Peter's knowledge in all aspects of British aviation is phenomenal and I count myself truly lucky to be a friend.

First published 2014

The History Press
The Mill, Brimscombe Port
Stroud, Gloucestershire, GL5 2QG
www.thehistorypress.co.uk

© Tony Buttler, 2014

British Library Cataloguing in Publication Data.
A catalogue record for this book is available from the British Library.

ISBN 978 0 7524 6746 7

Typesetting and origination by The History Press
Printed and bound in India by Nutech Print Services

CONTENTS

INTRODUCTION

I was very pleased indeed when The History Press asked me to put together a book about the Hawker Hunter jet fighter, one of my all-time favourite aeroplanes. The problem was finding a different approach to the subject which had not been covered before in the excellent volumes produced in the past by several authors. However, my strongest area of interest in aviation is the design and development of military aircraft and this aspect of the Hunter story, in comparison to its service record, has rarely been looked at in real depth. So the result is this new title, which looks at how the Hawker Hunter came into existence.

The early part of the story makes use of many original Air Staff and Ministry documents plus the day-to-day diaries for Hawker Aircraft Ltd, and this is followed up with coverage of the Hunter flight test programme, which provides a little insight into what flying the fighter was actually like. There is a very quick look at the type's service career and then a review of selected Hunters which were modified for various trials programmes, while an Appendix presents information for some proposed Hunter modifications and versions which were not adopted. The latter includes supersonic developments, the most important of which was the Hawker P.1083, which was ordered in prototype form but never flown. This book also takes the opportunity to bring together several batches of lovely official publicity or recognition photographs of the Hawker Hunter, which was and still is of course one of the most photogenic of all aeroplanes.

The Hawker Hunter F.1 first joined the Royal Air Force with No.43 Squadron in July 1954 and that proved to be the start of a long, successful and illustrious service career. However, by then the story of this famous aircraft had already stretched over seven years and it is that period, plus the airframe developments that followed, which form the core of this book. It has been a joy to write about this lovely aeroplane, something I have wanted to do for a long time!

Tony Buttler, Bretforton, May 2013.

ACKNOWLEDGEMENTS

In compiling this account I have made minimal reference to published or secondary sources, concentrating instead on primary documents. The main exception is the Flight Global Archive *www.flightglobal.com/pdfarchive* for *Flight* magazine issues covering mid-1950s Farnborough Shows. The Hawker Aircraft Ltd day-to-day diaries were supplied to me by the late Eric Morgan, while Hawker's own flight test reports and accounts come from the splendid Hawker archives held at the Brooklands Museum and administered by Chris Farara. Chris has also very kindly reviewed the text. The Boscombe Down and CFE reports, and many other Ministry and Government documents used for this work, were accessed in the AVIA and AIR files at the National Archives at Kew. Engine and airframe records and photographs for both Armstrong Siddeley and Rolls-Royce were searched on my behalf by David Birch, Peter Barnes, Peter Collins and other members of the Rolls-Royce Heritage Trust, with permission to use photos given by Simon Pank of Rolls-Royce Image Resource. My thanks to you all.

I must also thank former Hawker test pilot Duncan Simpson for answering questions about one-off Hunters, Bob Broad for putting together such a splendid account of flying the P.1109 version of the Hunter, and to Ian White and the EKCO Electronics website ekco-electronics.co.uk (Chris Poole) for help with further research on the P.1109 section. The Air-Britain airframe histories covering certain test-bed Hunters were also a most valuable source.

Once again, as so often in the past, my great friends Phil Butler and Peter Green have helped with a large number of the photos required for this book. Finally, thanks to Chrissy McMorris and the team at The History Press for turning my text and photos into this volume.

GLOSSARY

A&AEE	Aeroplane and Armament Experimental Establishment, Boscombe Down
AAM	Air-to-air missile
ACAS(OR)	Assistant Chief of the Air Staff (Operational Requirements)
AEW	Airborne Early Warning
AFC	Air Force Cross
AI	Air Interception
Air Ministry	British Government department of 1918 to 1964, which was responsible for managing the affairs of the RAF. It came under the political authority of the Secretary of State for Air
AVM	Air Vice Marshal
AWA	Armstrong Whitworth Aircraft
BLC	Boundary Layer Control
C(A)	Controller of Aircraft (UK)
CFE	Central Fighter Establishment
C-in-C	Commander-in-Chief
CO	Commanding Officer
CofG	Centre of Gravity
Critical Mach Number	Mach number at which an aircraft's controllability is first affected by compressibility, i.e. the point where shockwaves first appear
DARD	Director of Aircraft Research and Development (MoS post)
DFC	Distinguished Flying Cross
DGSR	Director General of Scientific Research (MoS post)
DGTD(A)	Director General of Technical Development (Air) (MoS post)
DMARD	Director of Military Aircraft Research and Development (MoS post)
DOR(A)	Director of Operational Requirements (Air)

DSO	Distinguished Service Order
DTD	Director of Technical Development (MoS post)
ETPS	Empire Test Pilots' School at Farnborough
IAS	Indicated Airspeed
IMN	Indicated Mach Number
incidence	Angle at which the wing (or tail) is set relative to the fuselage
JPT	Jet Pipe Temperature
MoD	Ministry of Defence – created in the late 1940s to co-ordinate the policy of the three Armed Services. In April 1964 the MoD was reconstituted to absorb the functions of the Air Ministry, the Admiralty and the War Office.
MoS	Ministry of Supply – created in August 1939 to provide stores for the RAF, Army and Navy. Disbanded and reconstituted as the Ministry of Aviation in 1959.
MU	Maintenance Unit
nm	nautical mile
OBE	Order of the British Empire
OR	Operational Requirement
PDRD(A)	Principal Director of Research and Development (Air) (MoS post)
PDSR(A)	Principal Director of Scientific Research (Air) (MoS post)
PDTD(A)	Principal Director of Technical Development (Air) (MoS post)
RAE	Royal Aircraft Establishment, Farnborough
RRE	Radar Research Establishment (Royal Radar Establishment from 1957)
RTO	Resident Technical Officer
SBAC	Society of British Aircraft Constructors
t/c	Thickness/chord ratio
transonic flight	The speed range either side of Mach 1.0 where an aircraft has both subsonic and supersonic airflow passing over it at the same time.
TRE	Telecommunications Research Establishment (RRE from 1953)
VI	Variable Incidence

one

A STAR IS BORN

July 2014 sees the 60th Anniversary of the service entry of the Hawker Hunter, one of the best fighters ever produced by the British aircraft industry and one of the best looking aeroplanes ever to grace the world's skies. The objective of this book is to highlight the story of how the Hunter jet fighter came into being, to catalogue the aircraft's development and to provide a detailed account of some of the flight testing that was accomplished to prepare it for service. In the process the main problems which troubled the programme along the way will be described.

The story of this RAF day interceptor fighter aircraft begins in January 1947 with the issuing of Specifications F.43/46 and F.44/46 for new day interceptor and night fighters respectively; F.43/46 was also covered by Operational Requirement OR.228. This was at a time when the dominance of the piston-powered fighter was coming to an end but the new jet-powered fighters were still feeling their way forward. At this time the RAF's front line jet equipment was the straight-wing Gloster Meteor and de Havilland Vampire (Britain's first and second jet fighters) but the advent of more advanced aerodynamic shapes in the form of the swept wing and delta wing would shortly provide much higher speeds and make these early types obsolete.

A beautiful photo of the first production Hunter F.Mk.1 WT555. (Air-Britain via Phil Butler)

Specifications F.43/46 and F.3/48

The day fighter's primary role was to be the destruction of high-speed, high-altitude bombers as soon as possible after they had been detected by ground radar. In fact, from a button start, the fighter had to reach 45,000ft (13,717m) in no more than 6 minutes. It was preferred that the new type would have swept wings and the maximum speed at 45,000ft (13,717m) had to be approximately 547 knots (630mph/1,014km/h) Mach 0.953 or, should there be difficulties in producing a swept wing layout, 500 knots (575mph/925km/h) for a more conventional design. The service ceiling had to be at least 50,000ft (15,240m) and this aircraft was intended to replace the Meteor. Designs were submitted by Gloster Aircraft, Hawker Aircraft and Supermarine, and Gloster's design was favoured at the Tender Design Conference held on 9 April 1947, but in due course Gloster's layout was revised and eventually emerged as the Javelin night fighter. In the meantime Hawker had tendered to the F.44/46 night fighter competition and was told that it would receive orders for its proposal, but then in September 1947 a decision was made to issue new specifications cancelling those already issued for day and night fighters.

In January 1948 the Air Staff stated a requirement for a high performance single-seat interceptor with four Aden guns (to be replaced later by a 4.5in (11.5cm) recoilless gun subsequently cancelled in November 1948) and radar ranging. This became the subject of Specification F.3/48, which replaced F.43/46 but was still part of OR.228. In the meantime it was considered that Hawker's night fighter design would have difficulty in meeting the new night fighter requirements outlined in F.4/48 (which replaced F.44/46). F.3/48 was issued in October 1948 and called for the provision of reheat – it was evident at this point that the MoS did not expect the aircraft to meet the performance requirements without reheat.

As a result Hawker was asked to submit a tender for a new single-seat day interceptor. In fact during 1947 and early 1948 the firm had assessed a number of solutions for interceptors and on 10 March these were brought together for discussion with the Ministry. By April a mock-up of the cockpit had been built, drawing office work commenced on 3 May, and further discussions were held until, by 25 June 1948, the design had stabilised sufficiently to enable a contract for three prototypes to be ordered. The Kingston-based company's ideas had been brought together in a design it called the P.1067 and the specified powerplant was a single Rolls-Royce Avon or Armstrong Siddeley Sapphire axial jet engine, at this stage with provision for reheat.

Hawker P.1052 and P.1081

In the meantime Hawker had been gathering data on swept wings using two research aeroplanes. The very successful straight-wing Sea Hawk naval fighter, first flown as the P.1040 in September 1947, had been the firm's first jet-powered aeroplane. Two P.1052 prototypes were also built which combined the Sea Hawk's fuselage with a swept wing but kept the type's straight tailplane and split bifurcated jet pipe to either side of the rear fuselage. The first example, VX272, made its maiden flight on 19 November 1948 and the second, VX279, followed on 13 April 1949. Both examples were powered by one 5,000lb (22.2kN) thrust Rolls-Royce Nene centrifugal jet engine. In the air the new type was liked by all of its pilots and was generally considered pleasant to fly.

To take the research further VX279 was subsequently rebuilt as the P.1081 with swept empennage and all through jet pipe and as such this attractive aeroplane bridged the gap between the earlier types and the Hunter. With its swept tail VX279 could provide knowledge for the effects of this new feature and on 11 May 1950 the airframe went back to Hawker's Experimental Shop to begin its conversion. In its new P.1081 guise, and at an all-up-weight of 11,048lb (5,011kg), VX279 made its second maiden flight on 19 June 1950 piloted by Hawker chief test pilot Sqn Ldr Trevor Sydney 'Wimpy' Wade AFC DFC. On 15 September, at a take-off weight of 12,350lb (5,602kg), VX279 achieved 635mph (1,022km/h) Mach 0.84 at sea level and 601mph (967km/h) Mach 0.89 at 30,000ft (9,144m); the sea level rate of climb was measured at 6,100ft/min (1,859m/min). VX279 was painted duck-egg green, a lovely colour used for several Hawker prototypes in the 1940s and '50s.

The manufacturer's flight testing was concluded in February 1951 and the covering report showed that the test pilots were delighted with the aircraft. Wade had just completed a trip to America where he had flown the North American F-86A and F-86E Sabre fighters and he concluded that the P.1081 was, certainly at altitude, a better all round fighter than the F-86. To date the maximum speed flown had been 648mph (1,043km/h) Indicated Airspeed (IAS) at low altitude (655mph/1,054km/h true airspeed) at which the handling characteristics had been satisfactory, although air conditions gave a moderately rough ride. In fact the performance of the aircraft at altitude had been severely limited by high engine jet pipe temperatures (JPT), which had been in evidence since an engine change and after the jet pipe had been lengthened. Hawker added that the P.1081 had now reached a most satisfactory stage of development. At its fully loaded fighter weight it had exceptional performance, virtually viceless handling characteristics, good manoeuvrability and a controllable Mach number range up to at least 0.94. In any one of these fields the P.1081 was considered superior to any other British aircraft now flying and its potential as a Service fighter was excellent. Tragically, however, before the aircraft could be handed over for its official trials, on 3 April VX279 was totally destroyed in a test flight accident and Wade was killed.

Some production plans were put together for the P.1081 when the possibility arose that an order for the type might come from Australia, but these came to naught. Had they done so, production examples of what was termed an interim interceptor fighter would have been powered by the 6,250lb (27.8kN) thrust Rolls-Royce RTa.1 Tay centrifugal engine. In fact the Hawker diary for

Boscombe Down photo of the Hawker P.1052 swept wing research aircraft. (Air-Britain via Phil Butler)

The second P.1052 was rebuilt with all-through jet pipe as the P.1081. The ground view shows this aircraft, VX279, at London Airport.

14 November 1950 reported that the Australian Government had decided to build the P.1067 instead of the P.1081, but this too came to nothing. In the end the P.1052 and P.1081 provided Hawker with plenty of swept wing data and information to work into its single-seat day fighter design.

There was some argument within the Ministry as to whether an interim P.1081-type of fighter should have been ordered for the RAF, a type that could have been in service before the Hunter. A document written by Air Cdr Silyn Roberts on 8 April 1954 noted how decisions made in 1946/47 affected the outcome. The first was that the RAF should exist on types then current until more advanced aircraft, such as the F.3/48 class fighter, became available. This ruled out any intensive development of swept wing fighters in the American F-86 Sabre class powered by the Nene or Tay engines with the consequent loss to the Service of that experience. The second was not to proceed with the development of flight at supersonic speed in a full-scale aircraft, instead relegating the research to model tests and tunnel investigations. This latter decision was at the time considered inevitable because Britain 'had no engine which could give the necessary intensity of thrust to achieve supersonic speed in level flight and resorting to diving was not considered a safe proposition on either side of the Atlantic'. Instead the full-scale research and flying centred on transonic types like the F.3/48.

In addition a June 1950 memo noted that, at the time F.3/48 and F.4/48 were being drawn up, Air Staff policy was clearly and emphatically to have an all-weather fighter force. However, at the same time it was felt that the possibility of having to tackle a few enemy bombers of very high performance, and to compete with enemy fighter cover, warranted a single-seat fighter of superior performance with good firepower but the simplest possible equipment. This latter concept was represented by the F.3/48 requirement. Although prototypes like the P.1052/P.1081 and the concurrent Supermarine Type 535 could have been put into production, the F.3/48 was not far behind and, as the Director of Operational Requirements (Air) noted, 'we simply cannot afford to re-equip with new fighters every two minutes'.

Finally, in May 1947 the Chiefs of the Air Staff had taken some decisions regarding future defence policy after concluding that the likelihood of war in the next five years was small, that the risk would increase gradually in the following five years, and would increase more steeply thereafter as the rehabilitation of Russia gathered momentum. It was clear that this country posed the most formidable threat to UK interests, especially from 1956 onwards. Then in June 1950 the Chiefs of Staff were forced to re-assess the threat in the light of war in Korea and concluded that total war was not inevitable, but that the moment of greatest danger in the next few years would probably be at around the latter half of 1952. As a result the acceleration of the introduction of the new day fighter into service became a high priority and, in addition, various interim aircraft were considered, namely the Hawker P.1052, P.1081, P.1062 (essentially a P.1081 with a T-tail) and the Supermarine 535. The Hawker projects were shelved because such an interim type would divert the firm's energy from the more immediate problem of getting the P.1067 into service quickly. Ultimately it was decided to order a development of the 535, the Supermarine Type 541 Swift, as an interim aircraft, but this went on to suffer a most difficult development with numerous problems.

Early problems with the Swift included poor low speed characteristics, poor manoeuvrability at high altitudes plus wing flexing at speed prior to aileron flutter at Mach 0.93. Later engine surge was discovered under certain flight conditions while the F.Mk.2 revealed a strong tendency to tighten in turns at height. In May 1954 all marks of Swift were grounded following a fatal accident, and in April 1955 all Mk.3, 4 and 6 aircraft were cancelled. The later FR.Mk.5 version and the F.Mk.7, which tested the Fairey Blue Sky (Fireflash) air-to-air missile, proved to be rather better aeroplanes.

Hawker P.1067

An early P.1067 drawing shows a nose intake with four cannon placed low down in a bulbous forward fuselage, but Hawker's full design proposal was the transonic circular fuselage P.1067 of August 1948. The small diameter fuselage was just sufficient to house a 6,500lb (28.9kN) thrust Rolls-Royce Avon axial turbojet with 20 per cent reheat (the Armstrong Siddeley Sapphire could be used as an alternative without much alteration to the aeroplane). A tail unit had been retained because it was felt that sufficient control and manoeuvrability was impossible without it. Indeed, there were doubts regarding the final position of the horizontal tailplane because of the high speeds at which this new aeroplane would fly, the large changes in trim and the possibility that the elevator might become ineffective. In fact the brochure offered alternative positions and Hawker's plan was to produce one prototype with the tail placed on top of the fin and a second with it positioned a little above the fuselage. Structurally the lower position had certain advantages, but from an aerodynamic point of view the 'T' position was considered to be much the better and would keep the tail out of the wing wake. A low tail would present fewer problems structurally but it would need to have greater area (52sq.ft/4.84sq.m rather than 47sq.ft/4.37sq.m for the T-tail) and it would shield the rudder and reduce its effectiveness. The delta tailplane allowed a one-piece elevator and was continuous from tip to tip.

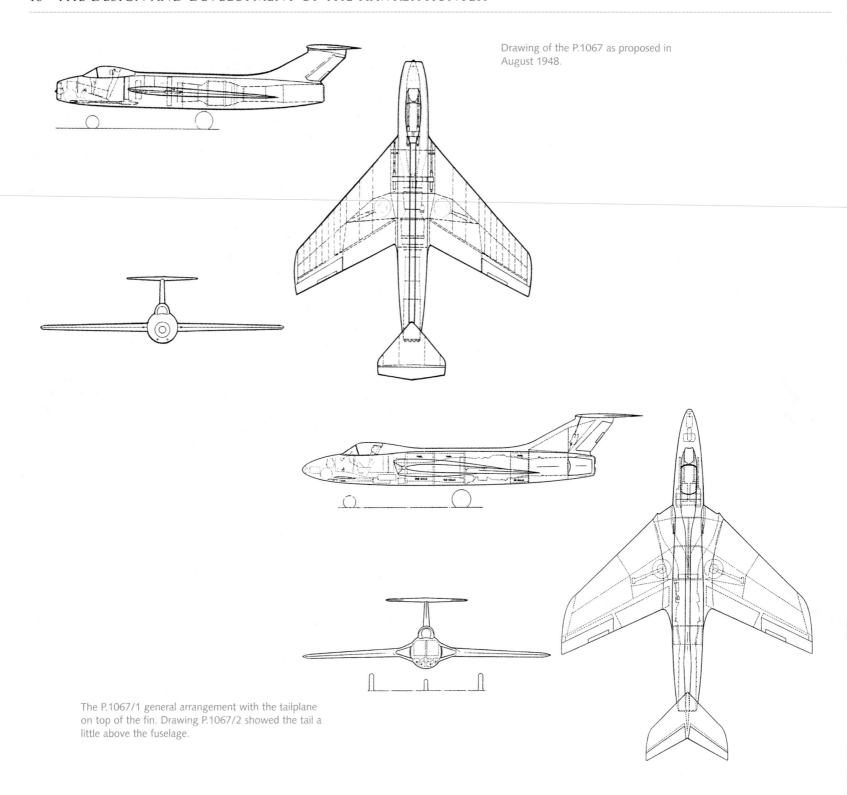

Drawing of the P.1067 as proposed in
August 1948.

The P.1067/1 general arrangement with the tailplane
on top of the fin. Drawing P.1067/2 showed the tail a
little above the fuselage.

Model of the T-tail P.1067 project.

The circular nose intake was split forward of the cockpit and converged just forward of the compressor entry to the engine. Two 20mm Hispano cannon were housed in the body with one more in each of the wing roots, provision was made for the substitution of two 30mm guns (dispensing with the wing root positions), and the radar ranging unit – including a fixed 10in (25.4cm) diameter 30 degrees view scanner – was to be housed in a dielectric fairing in the air intake entry. The wings, tail and rear fuselage were to be covered in thick gauge skin which in the former provided sufficient bending resistance without the necessity of using spars in the conventional manner (this method had been used on the Sea Hawk and P.1052 and had proved to be both stiff and light and gave a smooth lasting surface). The wings were swept 42.5 degrees on the quarter chord line, the thickness/chord (t/c) ratio was 8.5 per cent at the root and 10 per cent at the tip, and there were fairly large split landing flaps, the outer portions of which along with the upper surface flaps would serve as airbrakes.

The fuselage was pure monocoque with the thicker than usual skins again providing enough stiffness both in bending and torsion. Internal fuel capacity was 300gal (1,364lit) carried in the wings and in one small fuselage tank (which helped in achieving the minimum frontal area), and there was no provision for external tanks. The P.1067's span was 33ft 6in (10.22m), length 42ft 0in (12.80m), wing area 340sq.ft (31.62sq.m) and the all-up-weight with four 20mm cannon 12,970lb (5,883kg); with two 30mm cannon the all-up-weight was 12,870lb (5,838kg). When powered by a single Avon the estimated top speed was 710mph (1,142km/h) at sea level and 610mph (981km/h) at 40,000ft (12,192m), and the operational ceiling was approximately 53,000ft (16,154m).

Standard RAF armament since the early 1940s had been the hugely successful 20mm Hispano cannon, but by now this was no longer giving sufficient lethality against new modern aircraft structures. A replacement was required and the result was the 30mm Aden cannon, which became the RAF's standard weapon for its generation of transonic jet fighters, although initially there were 20mm and 30mm versions of the new gun.

Early in 1949 a major redesign of the P.1067 saw an increase in the fuselage diameter of 2in (5.1cm), which was made necessary by several changes including modifications to the fuel system. For technical reasons it had been decided not to proceed with integral fuel tanks and the fuel was therefore moved from the wing to the fuselage; the wing sweepback angle was also reduced. In addition, in January 1949 it was agreed that Avons should go in the first two prototypes while the third would have an Armstrong Siddeley

Photo showing a planview of the P.1081.

For comparison against the P.1081, this planview shows the first production Hunter WT555. The later aircraft's altogether sleeker form is most striking. (Air-Britain via Phil Butler)

Sapphire. By March the need to have a bigger radar, four 30mm cannon and an ejection seat in the forward fuselage made it clear that the air intake could no longer remain in the nose position and so this was switched to the wing roots, Hawker Aircraft's Harold Tuffen producing a new bifurcated wing root intake.

The part complete full size mock-up was officially inspected on 8 and 9 August 1949 by which time the design looked like the Hunter except for the T-tail. Afterwards the Air Staff asked for an improvement in the pilot's rear view and at the end of the month the mock-up was completed by the addition of its starboard wing. In October a decision was reached that the tailplane should now be in the low position, and in November it was decided to use a combination of strengthened landing flaps and dive recovery system to provide airbraking. In April 1950 the Director of Operational Requirements, keen to exploit the aircraft's full potential, asked the MoS if the airframe would be structurally safe for supersonic diving speeds up to Mach 1.2. The reply noted that the Specification called for design up to, but not beyond, Mach 1.0, that the aircraft appeared structurally safe but that control difficulties might be experienced. This speed requirement was eventually incorporated in OR.228 Issue 3 of January 1951.

At a meeting held at RAE in May 1950 Hawker and other fighter manufacturers were introduced to the Fairey Blue Sky (later Fireflash) air-to-air guided missile and the Ministry stated that the weapon was to be carried by the P.1067. In fact, apart from test aircraft XF310 discussed in Chapter 4, this never happened. The plan to have Blue Sky for the Hunter was dropped in February 1953 because of the firm's workload and because it would reduce the aircraft's endurance, but then a move was made to have the de Havilland Blue Jay (Firestreak) missile applied to the 50 degrees swept wing Hunter development (the P.1083 covered in Appendix 1). After the P.1083 had been cancelled, in July 1954 the Director of Operational Requirements (Air) declared that the Air Ministry had no requirement for Blue Jay on the Hunter.

On 20 October 1950, without any prototype having flown, Hawker received a production order for 200 aeroplanes with the first two Avon prototypes to be used to clear the F.Mk.1 version while the third with its Sapphire was earmarked to become the F.Mk.2 prototype. This step was part of an RAF expansion programme triggered by the outbreak of the Korean War. There was a worry that the Avon programme was overloaded (the engine was used by several new aircraft types) and there might not be enough units to meet P.1067 production commitments during 1953/54. In addition, an outlet was required for the Sapphire, the best use of the national industrial effort would be made if the Sapphire was used, and in 1951 Armstrong Siddeley's engine was thought to be capable of greater development than the Avon. Also in 1950 proposals were made for setting up a P.1067 production line at Gloster Aircraft; indeed, in February 1951, 150 examples were ordered from Armstrong Whitworth and another 150 from Gloster. In the end the Gloster line was never established (the firm's contract was cancelled to enable it to concentrate on the Javelin night fighter) and all Hunter production was undertaken by Hawker's Kingston upon Thames and Blackpool factories and by AWA at Coventry.

The production plans moved on to having one version of the fighter powered by the Avon RA.7 with reheat and the other with the basically more powerful but unreheated Sa.6. In fact an Air Staff memo dated 3 March 1952 noted that an Air Staff suggestion that the Sapphire Hunter should be cancelled would be an advantage from the operational point of view since all examples would have the same engine, and it was most unlikely that the aircraft's performance would be the same with both engines. On the other hand it was thought to be bad policy to have the same engine for all aircraft since a serious snag in that powerplant could ground every example. The same document noted that 'the Sapphire is a good engine, admittedly it is lagging behind the Avon in so far as build and Service experience is concerned but it has recently satisfactorily passed a type test at 7,500lb (33.3kN) thrust and has beaten the Avon in this respect'.

The Avon was designed from the start to provide 6,500lb (28.9kN) of thrust but it took several years and the solving of quite a few problems before this rating was achieved with the RA.3, which entered RAF service as the 100 Series Mk.101. In due course the thrust was increased and the RA.21/Mk.115 was rated at just over 8,000lb (35.6kN). Armstrong Siddeley Motors at Coventry took over the design and development of the F.9 Sapphire from its original designer Metropolitan-Vickers in 1947. At one stage the 7,200lb (32kN) thrust Sapphire was the world's most powerful jet engine and, despite having development problems of its own, it had a much better compressor than the Avon 100 series. In 1950 Rolls-Royce was able to take some of the best elements from the Sapphire's compressor and apply them in a full redesign of the Avon which became the 200 Series and which took the thrust rating to 10,000lb (44.4kN). The 200 Series subsequently went into the Hunter F.Mk.6.

In February 1951 a fourth prototype was ordered primarily for a developed engine, but this was subsequently turned into the P.1083 thin wing Hunter prototype described in Appendix 1. Also in February 1951 it was found necessary to shorten the Aden gun barrel by 14.5in (36.83cm) and this required an airframe change to the front mounting. The change in barrel length came from the decision to abandon the 20mm development and adopt the 30mm Aden gun as standard – the 20mm barrel length had been 57.5in

The Hunter production line in 1955. In the foreground, fifteen noses are made ready for attachment to their main fuselages.

(146.05cm) and the 30mm, 43.0in (109.22cm). At a meeting held on 21 February at Hawker, Sydney Camm was reported to be very peeved at such a late change in the Aden gun's design. The shorter barrels took away the P.1067's existing barrel support and a considerable amount of redesign was required to provide a replacement.

By the start of April 1950 the first aircraft's front fuselage structure was complete and its skinning had begun, and in October the outer wings had reached a fairly advanced state of construction. By the end of February 1951 all of the components for the first prototype were in their jigs, while the tailplane and elevator had been assembled together and fitted on the tail end for the first time on 26 February. The P.1067 bore a general resemblance to the P.1081 in that it had a swept back wing and tail unit and all-through jet pipe, but the fuselage was longer which gave the new aircraft a sleeker appearance than the rather squat P.1081. The long fairing which linked the rear cockpit coaming with the fin added to the impression of slenderness. A British national daily newspaper held a contest to name the new aircraft and its readers selected

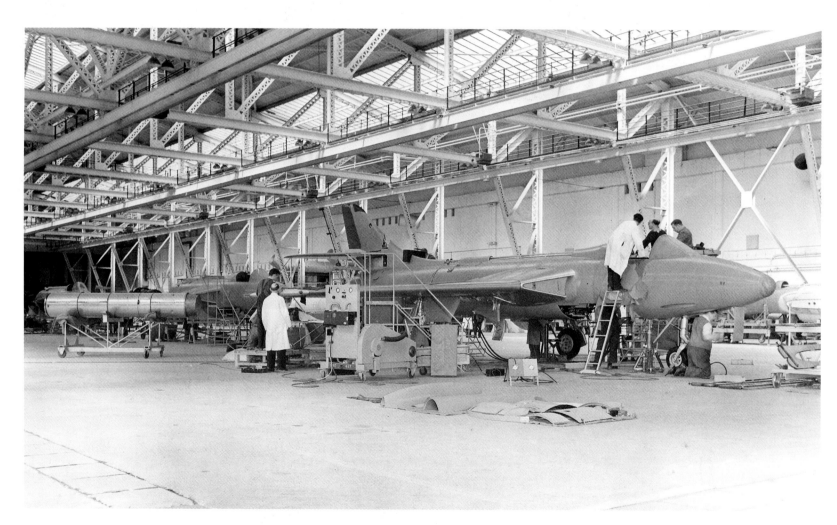

The Hunter final assembly line at Hawker's Blackpool factory.

Nose-angle views of very clean prototype WB188 in July 1951 (without guns) and a production Hunter with cannon and wing tanks. The former was one of the first P.1067 images released to the public.

'Demon' (a name previously used by Hawker for a biplane fighter), but the United States Navy had also picked this for its new McDonnell F3H interceptor and so the alternative 'Hunter' was chosen instead. The name, which had not previously been used for any other British aeroplane, was officially announced in the House of Commons in mid-March 1952 by Gp Capt the Hon G.R. Ward, the Undersecretary of State for Air.

The Avon-powered prototype WB188, again painted in duck-egg green livery, was the first to fly, on 20 July 1951. *The Aeroplane* magazine reported how at the SBAC Farnborough Show in September 1951 test pilot Neville Duke in WB188 reached the highest speeds achieved so far by any aeroplane flying at any SBAC Display. More than once he appeared to exceed the existing World Absolute Speed Record and at only tens of feet above the runway – and this was in an aircraft which had logged only 11 hours of flying prior to the Show (Hawker reported that 'useful development flying was accomplished during the demonstrations'). From October 1951 until 9 January 1952 WB188 was grounded for changes to be made to the fin and rudder (to try and cure some vibration experienced as flight testing had progressed to higher speeds), for the fitting of a production version of the RA.7 engine with variable swirl, and some strengthening to be made to the wing roots.

The second Avon prototype was WB195, which first became airborne on 5 May 1952 and was the first to carry the full four-30mm Aden gun pack. On 4 June it was demonstrated at West Raynham and WB195 also took part

The still very new WB188 pictured at the Farnborough Show in September 1951. (Peter Green Collection)

Two pictures of WB188 taken during flight trials. At this stage the prototype did not have airbrakes on the fuselage.

in the SBAC Show in September with WB188 being held in reserve. WB188 was returned to Hawker's Richmond Road works at Kingston on 3 December 1952 to begin a conversion to receive reheat as the Mk.3 (below), plus the fitting of wing tanks, while two days later WB195 was sent to Boscombe Down for assessment in response to a Fighter Command request that Central Fighter Establishment (CFE) pilots be allowed to make an early appraisal of the type. However, the second aircraft had to be returned on the 20th for an investigation into the cause of heavy vibration, which had been experienced after pull out from a dive at low altitude and high speed. This was later diagnosed as elevator flutter but the trials were not completed by Hawker until December 1953, WB195 having been employed on flutter investigation

for a whole year. The problem appeared to have been due to the effect of manufacturing variations in elevator skin thickness.

WB188 was eventually despatched to No.1 School of Technical Training at Halton where it was allotted ground instruction serial 7154M, and today it resides, still in its red Mk.3 livery, in the Tangmere Military Aviation Museum. WB195 arrived at RAE Farnborough on 26 October 1954 to be prepared for barrier trials; on 29 September 1955 it went by road from West Raynham to Henlow where it was allotted 7284M, and the aircraft was Struck Off Charge on 28 May 1959. However, it was not sold for scrap until 1967.

The third P.1067 prototype was the Sapphire-powered WB202, which first flew on 30 November 1952. This aircraft began ground firing gun trials on

The second P.1067 WB195 seen on display at Farnborough.

The third P.1067 was the Sapphire-powered WB202, which is also shown at Farnborough. (Peter Green Collection)

WB202 served as the prototype for the Hunter F.Mk.2. This version was taken off the Secret List in December 1952. The piston-powered two-seat Hawker Sea Fury T.Mk.20 visible in the background with its wings folded is VX283.

16 February 1953, with air firing trials commencing on 9 March. Also in March 1953 WB202 was fitted with a new engine and an extended fin to improve stability (the fin extension was successful and was later applied to all Hunters). WB202 took part in the 1954 Farnborough Show and on 22 December 1955 it arrived at Bedford for use in crash barrier trials. It was Struck Off Charge on 30 November 1957 for fire-fighting practice and scrapped at Bedford in 1960. Despite the development problems that the aircraft was to experience, late in 1952 the Air Council was told that the Americans regarded the Hunter as the finest fighter yet designed anywhere in the world, despite its military characteristics having yet to be tested.

Fighter Versions

Production orders for the Hunter were placed before any of the prototypes had flown and the first variants were the F.Mk.1 with an Avon RA.7 and F.Mk.2 with a Sapphire Sa.6. Armstrong Whitworth at Coventry built the latter while Hawker manufactured the Mk.1s. After a period of rundown in the industry, with the loss of facilities and skilled labour, putting several new types of British aircraft into production at roughly the same time presented many problems for manufacturing capability and capacity. For example the Hunter required some 3,250 tool designs and about 40,000 jigs, tools and fixtures had to be provided for. To try and break the bottleneck the British Government subsequently introduced the 'Superpriority' scheme, but in terms of speeding up production this was only partially successful since priority had to be allocated to so many items that the sub-contractors and suppliers were often unable to offer any measure of preference. At the same time of course, every effort was also being made to maintain aircraft exports.

The first production F.Mk.1 Hunter, WT555, first flew on 16 May 1953 from Dunsfold in the hands of Hawker test pilot Frank Murphy. The aircraft went to A&AEE for trials on 30 October and in fact the first twenty Mk.1s were all used for the development of equipment and installations. Intensive flying trials were conducted over twenty-one weeks of testing between 3 May and

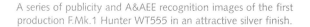
A series of publicity and A&AEE recognition images of the first production F.Mk.1 Hunter WT555 in an attractive silver finish.

The first F.Mk.2 built by Armstrong Whitworth at Coventry, WN888, was test-flown by AWA's chief test pilot E.G. Franklin and also by Frank Murphy of Hawker. (Peter Green)

control for landing. However, some confusion ensued which meant that the Hunters' approaches were stretched out and only two examples landed safely. Another flew into the ground killing its pilot, one belly-landed and the other four pilots ejected safely from their aircraft. Clearly the organisation at DFLS was not what it should have been but these Hunters were all out of fuel after only around 40 to 45 minutes flying. (Author's note: Official documents have so far given no clues as to why such low fuel levels and endurance had originally been accepted, either by the Air Ministry or Hawker.)

The first production model of the F.Mk.2, WN888 and the first Hunter from the Armstrong Whitworth production line, made its maiden flight at Baginton, Coventry, on 14 October 1953 piloted by AWA chief test pilot Eric Franklin; it was also flown by Hawker's Frank Murphy to allow a comparison to be made against the Mk.1 (see Chapter 2). Superficially the Mks.1 and 2 were almost identical, but there was one clear distinction – above the port side of the engine bay of both marks was a small flush intake and on the F.Mk.2 an oil-vent outlet could be seen just forward of and below this point. Again early machines were employed on trials. C(A) Release for the F.Mk.2 was given on 31 August 1954 with the same restrictions as the F.Mk.1.

The one-off Mk.3 (a paper written by a Hawker test pilot actually called it the F.Mk.3) was in fact prototype WB188 refitted with a reheated 9,500lb (42.2kN) thrust Avon RA.7R to serve as a trials machine both for the

25 September 1954 using three F.Mk.1 aircraft. Overall, the first production variant fell short of the performance requirements outlined in F.3/48, being a little down on endurance, ceiling and maximum speed and well down on the time from take off to 45,000ft (13,716m). C(A) Release to the Service for the Hunter F.Mk.1 was given on 1 July 1954 but with several limitations including armament firing restricted until trials were completed and a 4'g' limit at altitude to prevent tightening.

The early Hunters experienced problems which took time to solve. For example firing the guns caused surging in the Avon engine and there was a lack of fuel and endurance. These first two marks were quickly retired to training units after the fuel shortage was addressed by the arrival of two new versions, the Avon F.Mk.4 and Sapphire F.Mk.5 which both carried additional internal fuel and a drop tank under each wing. The lack of fuel in the early marks was highlighted by an incident on 8 February 1956 when eight F.Mk.1s from the Day Fighter Leader School (DFLS), part of the CFE, took off for a combat exercise. In due course the weather deteriorated at their base at West Raynham and so the formation had to recover to Marham using radar ground

Rear fuselage of F.Mk.2 WN909. Note the bullet fairing in the fin/tail junction.

P.1083 supersonic Hunter development described in Appendix 1 and for the development of reheat in general. Afterburning was developed to increase climb rate and acceleration but the facility provided very little improvement to the Hunter's level flight speed. As a result Sydney Camm reasoned that the extra weight, complexity and cost which reheat brought with it was for the Hunter not worth doing, and a better proposition would be a 'dry' engine of increased thrust, which in due course was satisfied by the Avon 200 series.

WB188 made its first flight with reheat fitted on 7 July 1953 and in this form, and painted scarlet red, the aircraft set a new world speed record of 727.6mph (1,170.7km/h) on 7 September 1953. The pilot who achieved the feat of bringing the record back to Britain after a lapse of six years was Sqn Ldr Neville Duke, DSO, OBE, DFC, AFC. The previous record holder had been a North American F-86D Sabre, which had reached 715.7mph (1,151.9km/h) on 16 July 1953, whilst the last British holder was the Gloster Meteor, which set a figure of 615.8mph (991.0km/h) in September 1946, that record having been broken in August 1947. The latest speed was calculated as a mean of four runs, two in each direction and flown over a 1.86-mile (3km) course established off the coast near Littlehampton in Sussex. In fact the four individual runs recorded speeds of 716.7mph (1,153.4km/h), 738.8mph (1,189.0km/h), 716.0mph (1,152.0km/h) and 738.6mph (1,188.7km/h).

For the record attempt Duke flew out of Tangmere and in all important respects the red-painted WB188 was a standard airframe, although features

WB188 in its Mk.3 form is attended to by Hawker staff during the speed record attempt.

This early F.Mk.4, WT703, is loaded with underwing bombs and tanks.

like the pointed nose and a curved fairing over the existing windscreen were not to be found in production aeroplanes. In this condition WB188 had a take-off weight when clean of 17,850lb (8,097kg) and carried 400gal (1,819lit) of internal fuel. At this moment it was the fastest aeroplane to have been built in Britain while its 1,000ft/min (305m/min) ceiling was given as 50,700ft (15,543m). However, the relatively chilly climate in Britain did not lend itself to the attainment of high speeds – a hotter venue was a better option because for a given Mach number the actual flight speed varied with the ambient air temperature. Indeed, the speed difference over the July 1953 figure established by the F-86D was just 11.9mph (19.1km/h) but that record was set at Muroc in America where the temperature was 105°F. The conditions along the south coast for Duke (73°F) meant that his 727.6mph (1,170.7km/h) figure equated to Mach 0.94. Had Duke flown WB188 to Mach 0.94 in the 105°F conditions of Muroc then that Mach number would have been equivalent to 750mph (1,207km/h). Consequently, when a Supermarine Swift broke WB188's record on 28 September 1953, setting a new figure of

735.7mph (1,184.0km/h), it did so at the rather warmer venue of Castel Idris in Libya. However, temperature conditions were only one element in setting these records – the limiting Mach number of the airframe was another factor.

On 19 September Duke in WB188 gained another world record, the 100km closed circuit with a speed of 709.2mph (1,141.1km/h), and here the weather conditions were even further from ideal – the temperature was below 60°F and there was rain, low cloud and poor light. The course began and ended at Dunsfold and entailed a 25-mile (40.2km) straight outward leg, followed by a 12-mile (19.3km) turn and another 25-mile (40.2km) straight leg home. In due course a Ministry review of the Hunter's progress stated that the speed records and the various demonstrations for which WB188 had attended had delayed and slowed up the Hunter's development work – the preparations had diverted the effort away from the attempt to clear the fighter for service.

The Mks.1 and 2 were succeeded on the production lines by the F.Mks.4 and 5 with increased fuel capacity in the wings instead of the rear fuselage tank and the ability to carry underwing stores including, as noted, auxiliary

Here WT703 carries tanks and rocket projectiles.

tanks; for this the aircraft had fixed fittings for universal pylons under the wings to take bombs, rockets or drop tanks. The first production F.Mk.4 was WT701 first flown from Dunsfold on 20 October 1954 and piloted by Frank Murphy. The first production Mk.4 with the later Avon RA.21/Mk.115 was WV385, delivered in August 1955. The RA.21 resulted from troubles with the Nimonic alloy used for the engine's turbine blades – the RA.7 could not be uprated as had been hoped to 8,000lb (35.6kN) of thrust by increasing the operating temperature, but instead had to be limited to 7,600lb (33.8kN). It was the RA.21 which introduced the 8,000lb (35.6kN) rating. The first production F.Mk.5 was WN954 built by AWA, which made its maiden flight on 19 October 1954.

A major advance was the P.1099 F.Mk.6, which introduced the more powerful Avon RA.23 (later RA.28) that finally gave the Hunter the full performance it deserved, and again there was more fuel. It was first planned that the thin-wing supersonic P.1083 should follow two years behind the

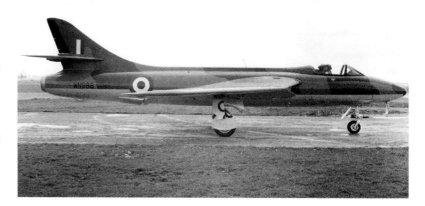

Production Hunter F.Mk.5 WN988. Note the airbrake under the rear fuselage.

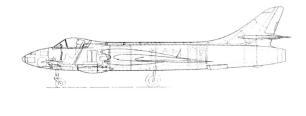

HAWKER HUNTER F.MK.6.
ROLLS ROYCE R.A. 28 ENGINE

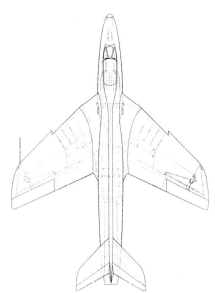

Manufacturer's drawing of the F.Mk.6.

The extended outer leading edge of the F.Mk.6 is shown by XF380 on 4 December 1956.

basic Hunter, but with the cancellation of this aircraft it was agreed with the Ministry on 12 August 1953 that Hawker should proceed with a large-engine non-reheat version of the Hunter. Work on the P.1099 started in the Drawing Office on the 24th and the wings and centre fuselage had been delivered to the Experimental Shop by 7 December 1953. The first example, serial XF833 which had the original P.1083 WN470 fuselage converted, flew on 22 January 1954 and was delivered to A&AEE on 8 February, where through engine failure it experienced a forced landing on the 20th. The aircraft was repaired but again experienced compressor blade failure on 29 April. Rolls-Royce conducted engine tests on XF833 at Dunsfold during the whole of May, but a series of engine failures due to compressor blade fatigue culminated in June with the Avon having to be de-rated from 10,500lb (46.7kN) to 10,000lb (44.4kN) thrust, and with steel stator and rear rotor blades being fitted. XF833 resumed flight testing on 20 July.

With an Avon of much higher thrust the F.Mk.6 was distinguished by a larger jet pipe, while the ailerons and elevators were fully powered. The Avon 203 conferred a marked increase in climb performance to the tropopause, but thereafter its beneficial effect was largely offset by the increased aircraft weight. The engine had excellent handling characteristics and the first production example was WW592, first flown on 23 May 1955, while the first production Mk.6 to be built by AWA was XF373. To many this version was

Lovely official photo of a Mk.6 also taken in 1956.

The P.1099/Mk.6 prototype was XF833, which is seen here fitted with rocket rails.

altogether regarded as a new aircraft and C(A) Release was given to the F.Mk.6 in May 1956. Here the restrictions included a maximum permissible weight for take off and all forms of flying of 17,500lb (7,938kg), while the maximum permissible speed (a strength limitation) except when firing the guns was 620 knots (714mph/1,149km/h) IAS. There were no limits on Mach number within this speed limit but gun firing was limited to similar speeds to earlier marks (see Chapter 2). Intentional spinning was prohibited. XF833 was later used for drag chute trials; on 21 April 1958 it went to RAE Bedford and on 17 November

1958 the airframe was moved by road to RAE Farnborough to undergo fatigue testing. It was Struck Off Charge on 31 October 1962.

Trainers

Two two-seat trainer versions of the Hunter with side-by-side seating were produced – the T.Mk.7 for the RAF and the Navy's T.Mk.8. Design work on a P.1101 two-seater with two guns commenced in July 1954 after a requirement

Comparison nose-angle views of WB188 and the T.Mk.7 two-seat prototype XJ615.
(Air-Britain via Phil Butler)

for a dual-trainer had been stated by the Air Ministry, and in September it was decided that the first aircraft should be based on the F.Mk.4. In January 1955 Specification T.157D & P was issued to cover the new version which called for two 30mm Adens, four rocket stations and the ability to carry two 1,000lb (454kg) bombs. One decision that had to be made was the choice of tandem or side-by-side seating – from the point of view of advanced flying training the former was better while the latter was the preferred when it came to weapons training and instrument flying; side-by-side seating was eventually selected.

The Mock-Up Conference was held on 4 March 1955 and the first P.1101, serial XJ615, first flew on 8 July 1955. By November flight trials had indicated that buffet from the cockpit hood was unacceptable and needed to be eliminated. As a result the prototype flew with a new (and final) shape of transparent hood on 30 May 1956 and the flying characteristics were now considered satisfactory, the aircraft being acceptably free from buffet and noise. The fairing behind the cockpit was now larger and of modified contour, but the investigations into curing buffet entirely, however, would continue for another twenty-one months, the final solution consisting of an almost insignificant spoiler on the rudder surface at 25 per cent chord in conjunction with trailing edge angle on the rudder tab. Aft of the intake the airframe was identical with the F.Mk.4, but forward of this point the nose was entirely new. Beneath the wider fuselage and cockpit were two streamlined fairings for the 30mm guns.

In June XJ615 completed its preliminary gun firing at high and low altitude giving satisfactory results, apart from engine surging which was present with the Avon 115 engine at high altitude (in July high altitude gun firing with the Avon 121 installed gave no surging at all). The aircraft was demonstrated at the Cologne Air Display on 3 June and on one flight the Commander-in-Chief (C-in-C) of the 2nd Tactical Air Force (the Earl of Bandon) flew as a passenger. A preview assessment was carried out by A&AEE pilots at Dunsfold on the 23rd and 24th and their impressions were generally favourable. At the 1956 SBAC Farnborough Show XJ615 was displayed by Bill Bedford with the greatly enlarged dorsal fairing aft of the hood, and resplendent in a two-tone red and white colour scheme, the aircraft having been repainted in August. The hood itself still conformed to the old smaller fairing line, and off the slight waist effect thus remaining a thick collar of vapour would form at high speed. On 20 October XJ615 was flown to Rome to be demonstrated to the Italian Air Staff, in the process setting a London–Rome record on the outward journey.

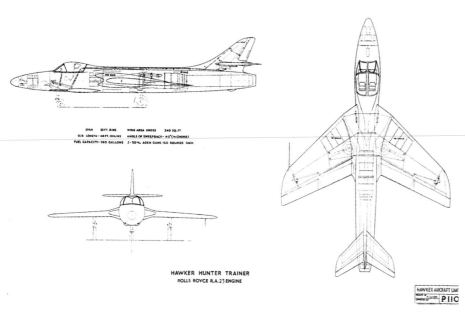

HAWKER HUNTER TRAINER
ROLLS ROYCE R.A.23 ENGINE

Manufacturer's drawing of the Hawker P.1101 two-seat trainer.

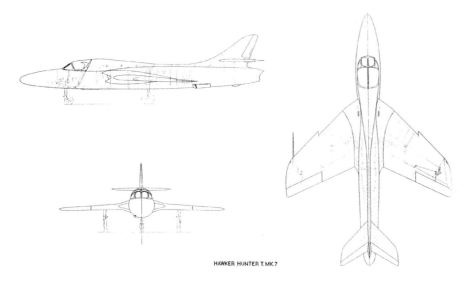

HAWKER HUNTER T.MK.7

Manufacturer's drawing of the T.Mk.7.

Line-up of T.Mk.7s, including XL586, which shows the different shape to their jet pipes compared to earlier marks of Hunter.

The T.Mk.7 prototype XJ615 pictured as first built and flown in July 1955 with an Avon 100 Series engine.

Manufacturer's photo showing XJ615 during an early test flight.

By the time of the SBAC Farnborough Show in September 1956 the canopy and rear fairing of XJ615 had been redesigned.

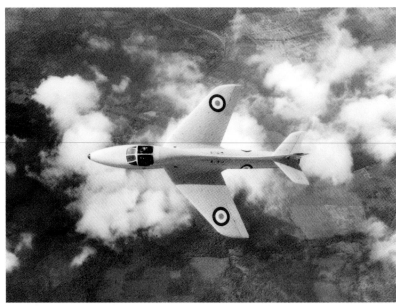

This series of photos of XJ615 was taken while the aircraft was in the hands of A&AEE Boscombe Down. (Air-Britain via Phil Butler)

During Farnborough several VIPs flew in XJ615 and towards the end of September representatives from Flying Training Command sampled the aircraft in order to evaluate its potential as a new advanced trainer. A design study for such a variant was submitted in October, the Hunter competing against a two-seat version of the Folland Gnat. An MoS and Air Staff design evaluation was carried out during November to assess the relative merits of the two types, Hawker understanding that the Gnat was very much favoured by Flying Training Command on the grounds of economy of operation and its relative simplicity. In May 1957 Hawker was told that the Air Staff had definitely decided against the Hunter and in favour of the Gnat, but also that the Ministry were not in agreement with this choice. After the Gnat had been ordered, in March 1958 chief designer Sydney Camm and his test pilots launched an intensive propaganda directed at the Ministry and Air Staff pointing out the desirability of having the Hunter Advanced Trainer instead of the Gnat. The arguments over the merits of the two types continued with strong support for the Gnat, despite recent Aden gun trials with Folland's aircraft having revealed some serious problems.

In January 1958 Hawker began a major effort to produce a private venture Advanced Trainer airframe for demonstration purposes, including asking for support from Rolls-Royce (this formed part of the effort to interest the Air Staff). In February and March enquiries were received regarding the cost of converting former Mk.4 and Mk.6 airframes into advanced trainers, and at the beginning of June the Experimental Department began to assemble the aircraft which eventually received the civilian registration G-APUX. This first flew on 12 August and was demonstrated by Bill Bedford at the Farnborough Show, including using full smoke emission during a multi-spin turn. A month later G-APUX returned from a successful demonstration tour of Switzerland, by which time the first two-seater for Peru had flown (Hunter exports were by now building up). In March 1960 G-APUX went to Lossiemouth for evaluation as a naval trainer and this aircraft went on to complete numerous demonstrations and displays over several years.

An order for trainers was received by Hawker's Blackpool factory on 12 March 1956, and on 31 May the firm was officially notified that the second prototype two-seater could proceed based on an F.Mk.6 rear fuselage. This

Two-seat Hunter G-APUX was a Hawker private venture advanced trainer and was used for demonstration tours to help sell the aircraft abroad. It was painted in an attractive red and white colour scheme and is seen equipped with 100gal (455lit) underwing tanks.

G-APUX trails smoke for the publicity camera. Indeed smoke featured heavily in the aircraft's display routines. Note the twin cannon and the huge 230gal (1,046lit) drop tanks which were on trial when the photo was taken.

The second P.1101 prototype was XJ627, which had a 200 Series Avon.

was XJ627 which first flew on 17 November 1956. It had the production windscreen and cockpit hood arrangement and its flying characteristics were found to be generally similar to the first machine, although the noise level was slightly higher. However, in December and into January 1957 rudder vibration was experienced in both prototypes during the pull out from supersonic dives. In May XJ627 was flown satisfactorily without the hood up to approximately 691mph (1,112km/h) IAS.

In June 1957 XJ615 was delivered to Boscombe Down to begin intensive armament trials (which were a success and lasted for the rest of the year) while XJ627 returned from attending the Paris Show. The latter was eventually used by A&AEE for radio and radar trials while in January 1958 XJ615 moved on to spinning trials. These were completed by Hawker on 19 March. In April 1959 this airframe went to the Empire Test Pilots' School (ETPS) at Farnborough for use on performance and handling instruction work, including spinning. XJ615 was Struck Off Charge on 29 September 1964 having been written off following a fatal crash on 24 June. During 1958 XJ627 was employed on ejector-seat trials including a visit to Martin-Baker at Chalgrove in October; in 1968 it was sold back to Hawker Siddeley and, after overhaul, was sold to

Chile. The first production T.Mk.7 was XL563, which made its maiden flight on 11 October 1957 and went to A&AEE to undergo C(A) Release trials on 19 December. C(A) Release for Service for the Mk.7 was issued on 22 May 1958. Two production two-seaters with various external stores attended the SBAC Show at Farnborough during the first week of September.

For the Navy's aircraft the requested equipment changes included a 1½'g' arrestor hook to cater for airfield emergency landings and in July 1957 the arrestor hook was tested on an F.Mk.6 at RAE Bedford. By July 1957 Hawker had instructed that five T.Mk.7s should be delivered to the Navy with one incorporating all of the Navy's modifications as a trials aircraft for A&AEE

approval. It was anticipated that the Navy would be ordering thirty Mk.7s using converted ex-RAF F.Mk.4 airframes. The first production T.Mk.8 was WW664 first flown on 3 March 1958 and satisfactory arrestor hook trials took place at RAE Bedford in April.

On 11 November 1955 Hawker completed proposal brochures for two-seat all-weather fighter versions complete with a search radar and wingtip fuel tanks called respectively the P.1114 and P.1115. Design work on these began in January 1956 and tunnel testing (at RAE) was completed in April, but neither type was ordered.

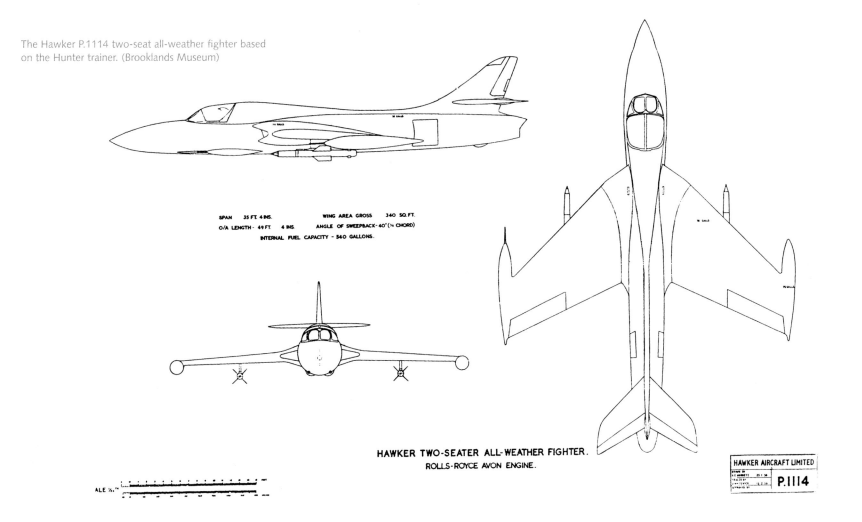

The Hawker P.1114 two-seat all-weather fighter based on the Hunter trainer. (Brooklands Museum)

SPAN   35 FT. 4 INS.
O/A LENGTH - 49 FT.   4 INS.
WING AREA GROSS   340 SQ.FT.
ANGLE OF SWEEPBACK - 40° (¼ CHORD)
INTERNAL FUEL CAPACITY - 540 GALLONS.

HAWKER TWO-SEATER ALL-WEATHER FIGHTER.
ROLLS-ROYCE AVON ENGINE.

HAWKER AIRCRAFT LIMITED
P.1114

The Hawker P.1115 two-seat all-weather fighter project also used the Hunter trainer airframe as a basis. (Brooklands Museum)

SPAN   33 FT 8 INS   WING AREA GROSS   340 SQ FT
O/A LENGTH - 50 FT. 6 INS.   ANGLE OF SWEEPBACK - 40°(¼ CHORD)
FUEL CAPACITY - 540 GALLONS   2 - 30 mm ADEN GUNS 150 ROUNDS EACH

HAWKER TWO-SEATER ALL-WEATHER FIGHTER
ARMSTRONG SIDDELEY SAPPHIRE Sa.6 ENGINE

HAWKER AIRCRAFT LTD

P.1115

Later Developments

Nearly 130 F.Mk.6s were later converted to FGA.Mk.9 standard with the ability to carry more ground attack weaponry, another thirty-three were refitted with cameras to become reconnaissance FR.Mk.10s, while one more example was converted into a two-seat T.Mk.12 trials machine which was ordered by the Ministry of Supply on behalf of RAE Farnborough. The first Mk.9 to fly as such was the 'prototype' XG135 on 3 July 1959 and the first Mk.10 was XF429 first flown in this form on 7 November 1958.

In terms of new-build aircraft for British use only, the total number of Hunters to be manufactured was three P.1067, one P.1099/F.Mk.6 and two P.1101 prototypes, 139 F.Mk.1, 45 F.Mk.2, 349 F.Mk.4, 105 F.Mk.5, 383 F.Mk.6

and 45 T.Mk.7 for the RAF, plus another 10 T.Mk.8 for the Royal Navy. The British factories also built large numbers for export (for example 120 Mk.4s as F.Mk.50s for Sweden) and refurbishment work kept Hawker's employees busy for a long time after that. Many ex-RAF airframes were eventually refurbished and sold abroad, but the manufacture for overseas markets was also met by separate production lines at Fairey-SABCA and Fokker-Aviolanda for Belgium and Holland. The grand total of Hawker Hunter production reached 1,972 aircraft. Apart from the Mk.6s upgraded to Mk.9 and 10 standard many more Hunters, particularly surplus Mk.4s, were rebuilt in various forms and this included forty Mk.4s into GA.Mk.11s fitted with hooks but without guns to provide training for the Royal Navy. A good number of single-seaters were also converted into two-seat versions for the RAF, Navy and overseas.

Hunter XE587 was an F.Mk.6 upgraded to FGA.Mk.9 standard but which in fact was never redesignated as such. It was photographed in 1957. (Peter Green Collection)

The 'prototype' FR.Mk.10 was XF429 rebuilt from an F.Mk.6.

The Hunter was to be late on its production dates because of teething troubles which, although not as serious as those suffered by the rival Supermarine Swift, caused more difficulty both on account of the cramped construction of the aircraft and because the design team at Hawker was (in 1953) considered by the Air Staff to be weaker than that at Supermarine (this quotation comes from an April 1953 memo written by Air Vice Marshal Geoffrey Tuttle, the Assistant Chief of the Air Staff (Operational Requirements)). Nevertheless,

right through from drawing board to roll-out the Hunter seemed to be a pilot's aeroplane. Aircrew would find that the cockpit felt right and it was small enough to make them feel part of the aeroplane, being slightly narrow at the shoulders giving the snug effect which was common to British fighters. But any new aeroplane needed thorough testing and it is time to look at the Hunter's flight test programmes.

WV380 was an F.Mk.4 Hunter upgraded to GA.Mk.11 standard for the Royal Navy. As such it is pictured in flight in 1962.

two

FLIGHT TESTING and DEVELOPMENT ISSUES

The flight test programme for any new aircraft has to be long and thorough to try and ensure that no weaknesses get through when the type reaches Service use. For the Hawker Hunter, with a number of different versions and then a variety of development problems, this work took some years. Being a military type, the early manufacturer's testing was followed by official trials at the Aeroplane and Armament Experimental Establishment (A&AEE) at Boscombe Down in Wiltshire. This chapter opens with a selection of Hawker flight reports before moving on to A&AEE's assessments and the problems uncovered during development flying.

Manufacturer's Flight Trials

The first Hawker P.1067 WB188 was transferred by road from the company's experimental shop to Boscombe Down on 27 June; the first engine run was made on 1 July; the aircraft was weighed on 3 July and the first taxi runs were carried out on 8 July, when some brake trouble was experienced, but a speed of 115mph (185km/h) was reached on the second run. More taxi trials were performed on the 13th and WB188 then made its maiden flight on 20 July 1951 with Hawker chief test pilot Neville Duke in the cockpit, the successful sortie lasting some 50 minutes. Full fuel was carried for a take-off weight of 15,465lb (7,015kg) and brief general handling was explored over a limited speed range up to 300 knots (345mph/556km/h). Some lateral oscillation was experienced but there were no serious problems. From the handling point of view, when flying at 15,000ft (4,572m) the ailerons were very light, responsive and most effective (in fact so much so that any slight control movement caused

It never seemed to matter from which angle the aircraft was photographed because the Hawker Hunter's distinct shape easily gave away the type's identity. This aircraft from No.2 Squadron was photographed from the nose camera of another FR.Mk.10. (Martyn Chorlton)

a disproportionate response from the aircraft), the elevator was very heavy but effective with good response, and the rudder was moderately heavy and fairly ineffective, although responsive. WB188 was very easy to trim longitudinally.

After five sorties from Boscombe WB188 was flown to Farnborough on 10 August where company testing was carried out until Hawker had completed moving its flight test facilities from Langley airfield to Dunsfold in Surrey on 7 September 1951. During October the testing of WB188 by Hawker's pilots concentrated on performance measurement and in all over 9 hours flying was achieved producing results which were considered to be very satisfactory and well up to expectation. In February 1952 a height limit of 40,000ft (12,192m) was removed to expand the development flying while in May it was decided not to send WB188 to Boscombe for pre-view flight trials as originally planned but instead to have two pilots despatched to the firm. The visitors had two flights each and the main criticisms they raised were the lack of airbrakes, poor longitudinal control and high stick forces at high IAS.

More photos of the beautiful first prototype WB188 in its duck-egg green colour scheme. The nose angle view is a Hawker photo but the rest of these images came from the A&AEE archives. (Air-Britain via Phil Butler)

The next important landmark was the cure of some tail-end vibration in WB188 by the introduction of a rear junction fairing and, as a result, transonic and supersonic flight was achieved for the first time on 24 June 1952. In fact, although early flying in WB188 had very quickly seen the aeroplane in the region of Mach 1.0 (a Ministry review states that Mach 1.0 was achieved in March) this could not be confirmed and any further advances were precluded by the tail-end buffet and vibration. The efforts to try and cure the problem embraced spoilers on the fin, a short rudder, an additional dorsal fin, and modified rear-end shapes in the region of the jet pipe, but the final solution came in the form of a bullet fairing fitted to the fin and tailplane trailing-edge junction. Although the first flight where supersonic speed was confirmed took place on 24 June, in fact because of the vibration difficulties it was quite likely that WB188 had broken through the sound barrier during any of the flights made after 6 June. The first supersonic demonstration to the public took place at the International Air Display at Melsbroek, Brussels, on 10 July 1952, while that year's Farnborough Show in September saw plenty of sonic bangs!

Hawker's assessment of Armstrong Whitworth-built F.Mk.2 WN888 was made by Frank Murphy in two flights on 21 and 22 October 1953. The take-off weight with 314gal (1,428lit) of fuel was 15,174lb (6,883kg) and Murphy commented in particular on the aircraft's behaviour in transonic dives up to Mach 0.98 and 1.01 respectively. Throughout the dive the aircraft rocked laterally and at transonic speeds (Mach 0.96 to 0.99) it was thought that the aircraft was rather lighter laterally than Dunsfold production aeroplanes. The ailerons at altitude were good and were considerably more effective than usual at 0.97 to 0.99 Indicated Mach Number (IMN). The maximum speed reached from a slight dive at 500ft (152m) was approximately 702/708mph (1,130/1,139km/h) and Mach 0.935 and at this condition the drag rise was apparent. There was also no directional change of trim as had been experienced on some production F.Mk.1 aircraft, while at high IAS the ailerons were normal or slightly heavier. At full throttle and high IAS there was more noise than that experienced in Mk.1 aircraft and this was thought to be a characteristic of the Sapphire installation. Overall, the aircraft generally achieved the same standard as production Mk.1 machines and a check of the recorded figures showed that these were very similar to the Avon-powered type, taking into account the different engine installation and power.

Fabulous action photo of the third P.1067 prototype WB202.

On 9 February 1954 Frank Murphy took F.Mk.6 prototype XF933 on a 30-minute flight for general handling tests and clearance at high Mach number, indicated airspeed and acceleration. He reported that on take off with full-power ailerons with spring feel there was considerably less tendency to lateral rocking after becoming airborne. A 30 degrees dive was initiated at Mach 0.9 and 43,000ft (13,106m) with the angle being increased gradually to a maximum of about 45 degrees. There was some rudder movement at approximately 0.96 IMN and a transitory wing low effect at about the same Mach number, such as had often been experienced on production F.Mk.1 aircraft. The characteristic forward stick movement occurred at 0.98 IMN and the Mach number increased comparatively slowly to 1.01 IMN. Subsequently, the Mach number increased rapidly to 1.13 IMN at which point a suggestion of a further elevator shock-wave effect was felt on the stick. Recovery was finally commenced, principally on the elevator together with some use of the tailplane, at 1.15 IMN and 30,000ft (9,144m), and, with a gentle pull out at 1.5 to 2.0'g', level flight was regained at 1.02 to 1.03 IMN at 20,000ft (6,096m). Murphy reported that the elevators were disappointing, the large increase in power appearing to have brought about a comparatively small improvement in fore and aft manoeuvrability. Prior to this flight the highest altitude recorded in XF933 had been 53,000ft (16,154m).

A&AEE Boscombe Down Flight Trials

The Hunter was first flown by an A&AEE pilot out of Boscombe Down on 11 December 1952, in fact by Wg Cdr Balmforth. WB195 was the aeroplane that first went to Boscombe but after only two weeks it had to be returned to Hawker because of heavy vibration experienced from the pull out of a dive at low level. On the credit side Balmforth reported that the Hunter had an impressive performance by present standards and was able to fly at and above the speed of sound, while at low speeds the fighter had a creditably docile behaviour. However, at Mach numbers in excess of about 0.75 IMN, which was in the probable combat zone, the rate of roll was unacceptably low below 15,000 to 20,000ft (4,572 to 6,096m) and needed to be increased to the region of 180 degrees/sec. In addition, all of the controls needed lightening considerably and indeed the heaviness of the elevator and large trim changes at high Mach number would seriously restrict the offensive use of the aircraft above about 0.93 IMN. This suggested that urgent consideration be given to some form of 'flying tail'. On top of this the airbrakes were described as unsatisfactory – satisfactory airbrakes were essential and some undamped and uncontrollable lateral oscillation at low and moderate IAS needed to be eliminated.

In April 1957 A&AEE completed a summary of the Hunter's development history based on its testing of various marks of the fighter between November 1953 and March 1957. This concluded that the development of the Hunter F.Mk.1 to the F.Mk.6 in its fully modified and equipped state had produced a considerable improvement in the fighter's handling characteristics. The aircraft's performance at 45,000ft (13,716m) included Mach 0.93 level speed and 3.25nm (6.02km) level turn radius, and A&AEE commented that, in terms of climb performance and manoeuvring capability which were very credible indeed, the Hunter compared well with the best of any known contemporary day fighters other than those which were fully supersonic. In its final form it was well suited to the air superiority and ground attack roles, and its performance made the aircraft satisfactory for the current threat and early warning environment.

A&AEE's appreciation of the F.Mk.1 had referred to good performance, docile transonic performance, excellent aileron control in power and good cockpit layout, but criticised longitudinal instability and control at high speeds, heaviness of aileron control in manual, liability to engine surge, liability to fuel unbalance, inadequacy of airbrake and tightening in turns. The good features were also marred, however, by rapid pitch-up in some manoeuvres at the higher subsonic Mach numbers and by the elevator becoming excessively heavy at such Mach numbers. The pitch-up, which was not preceded by adequate warning, restricted manoeuvring for aiming and also, at moderate altitudes, introduced structural hazards.

The F.Mk.1 was cleared by the establishment for Service use (familiarisation in the interceptor role) in June 1954. At that date the type represented a considerable advance in performance over its predecessors in the RAF but it exhibited several deficiencies both with regard to its handling characteristics and with regard to the state of development of operational equipment. The major deficiencies, either known at the time or revealed subsequently in testing, were:

1. Inadequate longitudinal control.
2. Pitch-up (the pitch-up phenomenon was in fact discovered by A&AEE).
3. Marginal engine handling characteristics.
4. Severe engine surge and aircraft nosing down problems with gun firing.
5. Severe structural and mechanical problems with gun firing.
6. Marginal handling characteristics in approaches using manual aileron control in turbulent conditions.

The operational deficiencies at the time of the initial release involved no gun firing clearance, no radar ranging, and no provision for the carriage of external stores. In due course the complete series of subsequent marks had successively been released, and clearance given on some marks for the carriage of external stores, and the extension of the role to cover ground attack duties.

The modifications which had been introduced were:

1.   Longitudinal control – full powered elevator, then follow up tailplane.
2.   Wing planform – extended outer wing leading edge.
3.   Lateral control – aileron spring feel trimmer, increase power aileron jacks, then reduced aileron gearing in manual.
4.   Directional control in aiming – yaw damper.
5.   Gun firing and engine handling – Avon 121 fitted retrospectively to Mks.1 and 4. Avon 203 fitted to Mk.6.
6.   Gun firing effect on aiming – deflectors fitted on gun blast tube.

The fully powered elevator of the Mk.6 conferred a marked improvement in handling qualities below 0.96 IMN over the boosted elevators of earlier marks. Aiming was possible up to 0.93 IMN, and above 0.98 IMN elevator jack stalling limited the 'g' available to about 1.9. The electric flying tail was a

Gloster Aircraft photographer Russell Adams had a reputation for taking pictures of aeroplanes as they performed a loop, the camera aircraft flying alongside its subject. This pair of images by Adams shows WB195 in 1952, the second P.1067 prototype and the first to be tested by A&AEE, Boscombe Down. (Jet Age Museum)

commendably simple modification which, although slow in operation, greatly improved the high altitude handling qualities and manoeuvring potential of the aircraft particularly at supersonic speeds, where 3.8'g' was available at a typical Centre of Gravity (CofG) position with the 3,500lb (1,588kg) elevator jack installed. Aiming was possible up to 0.98 IMN. Its rate of operation was satisfactory for general use and fighter to bomber attack but its adequacy for fighter-to-fighter day combat could not be so readily assessed. The development of longitudinal control had resulted in three separate systems being incorporated in Service variants:

1. Power boost in the F.Mks.1, 2, 4 and 5.
2. Full power in production F.Mk.6s and retrospective modification to Mks.4 and 5.
3. Electric flying tail in later Mk.6 production aircraft and retrospective modification to Mk.4 and early Mk.6 aircraft.

The stick forces of the power boost system were far too heavy and led to the prohibition of ground attack manoeuvres in Mk.4 and 5 aircraft.

The Mk.6's extended leading edge raised the buffet boundaries and useable 'g' by appreciable amounts, and it had alleviated the sharp uncontrollable pitch-up which as noted was a feature with the plain wing on the Mk.1. Pitch-up tendencies remained above about 0.90 IMN but were at all times controllable, while a secondary effect had been an improvement in the approach characteristics. The introduction of the Avon 121 engine on the Mks.1 and 4 and the 203 in the Mk.6 had brought the engine handling characteristics on these versions to a satisfactory level with regard to surges induced by throttle movement, by flight at high altitude and incidence, and by firing the guns. With either of these engines, and the Sa.6 series in the Mks.2 and 5, unrestricted gun firing was permissible.

Developments in performance had generally been of a minor nature, although a significant increase in the operational radius and ferry range were conferred by the extra internal fuel of later marks. However, the level speed performance did mean that targets flying 10 per cent faster could not be intercepted satisfactorily, with the present pursuit course short range gun armament in any but the most favourable circumstances. The four Aden fitting had commendable firepower and was neat and functioned satisfactorily, but it had brought in its train an accumulation of troubles which had required a prodigious development effort to overcome. Having gone through the A&AEE review, the most serious development problems experienced by the various marks of Hawker Hunter can now be discussed in turn.

Airbrakes

The Hunter was originally designed to use its landing flaps for airbrakes in the same way that Hawker had previously and satisfactorily done with the flap type of brake on the earlier Sea Hawk naval jet fighter. However, in early 1951 the firm was experiencing great difficulty in finding an airbrake which did not produce a change of trim. By September 1951, two months after WB188's first flight, flight trials had shown that the landing flap airbrakes, with dive recovery flaps to offset trim change, were unsatisfactory and the firm had begun to consider improvements. As a result flight investigations were made in May 1952 of a new airbrake scheme fitted on WB195 which consisted of a small fixed upper flap on the wing top surface above the landing flap and the preliminary tests showed that this arrangement was quite promising, but in the end it proved unsuccessful.

Sydney Camm reported on 28 November 1952 that the airbrakes were still ineffective at high speeds and caused large and possibly unacceptable changes of trim in the landing configuration. It was quite possible that the Service would not accept the Hunter with the existing airbrakes and further ideas suggested introducing a slotted finger flap arrangement, a rear fuselage brake, or an interconnection between the flaps and tail which would balance out changes of trim. In due course A&AEE reported that its pilots did not like the airbrakes on WB195, saying that they were unsatisfactory and unacceptable (excessive changes of trim occurred when the brakes were used at moderate and high IAS), and action to improve them became a high priority.

In February 1953 Hawker reported that it was going to try fuselage airbrakes and also to improve the existing flap brakes. In March the firm tried dividing the landing flaps into two parts and operating only half for airbraking. Early in April the Ministry's Resident Technical Officer (RTO) at Hawker reported that, although greatly improved, the modified flap brakes were still some way from being satisfactory. Then on the 27th the firm stated that it did not intend to fit fuselage brakes if an alternative could be found since not only was their affect on the CofG serious but they also involved a large and difficult change to production aircraft. Tests on WB202 with the single joint brake were made on 24 April 1953, but during the spring of that year the most troublesome feature of the Hunter was elevator flutter, in early summer it was reheat (both below), and in late summer there was a problem with landing distance. All of these tended to push the airbrake question into the background. Then, shortly after mid-summer, a decision was taken not to fit reheat, which made the fitting of fuselage airbrakes easier, and Hawker now went ahead with more enthusiasm. At this time it was thought that while fuselage brakes might give the ultimate solution, the aircraft would be just acceptable with the modified flap brakes. Frustratingly, airbrakes comprising the landing flap with an auxiliary trailing edge portion were tested on 29 June 1953 and gave poor results.

The fuselage brakes were designed to be fitted at the extreme aft position and near the jet pipe. They were, however, first fitted to a prototype, which had a jet pipe some 18in (45.72m) shorter than production aeroplanes, i.e. the pipe was 18in (45.72cm) closer to the brakes. Flight trials were carried out from 1 July and into the autumn of 1953, and it was found that these brakes gave considerable buffet and an unacceptable nose down change of trim. This was thought to be due to the proximity of the jet efflux and so a redesign had the brakes moved about 12in (30.48cm) further forward. While this was being carried out on WB188 (in September–November 1953, full power ailerons and spring feel to the ailerons and elevator were fitted at the same time), a Hunter went to Boscombe Down for acceptance trials. This was the first time that A&AEE had flown the type since flutter trouble had been discovered on WB195 in December 1952 and the pilots reported that the landing-flap-type airbrakes (the interconnection of flaps and elevator) were unacceptable, stating that the aircraft would be drastically restricted in its operational role and it was doubtful if it could be considered safe for release. A&AEE added that at high speed and low altitude the use of these brakes was likely to be dangerous.

The unsatisfactory results of the rear-fuselage format brought an urgent programme to solve the problem and ensure that the Hunter would get its C(A) Release. The modified 'moved-forward' airbrakes were first tested by Hawker on 20 November 1953 but were no better than before, prompting the Air Staff later that month to declare that it would not accept the Hunter unless the aircraft was provided with effective airbrakes that could be used safely throughout its speed and Mach number range. In fact this was a minimum requirement and the Air Staff attached great importance to improving the brakes beyond this standard so that they could be used in combat without producing changes of trim or attitude that would prevent the pilot keeping his sights on the target.

It was therefore agreed that Hawker would proceed with the following trial installations as a matter of the greatest urgency, utilising all available production aircraft for the purpose:

(a) Trials of the fuselage brakes, with the holes in the fuselage behind the brakes filled in, and with horizontal fins fitted to the top and bottom of the brakes and to the fuselage opposite the brakes. The object of this modification was to do away with

the turbulence due to holes in the fuselage, and to prevent the airflow from the brakes interfering with the tailplane.

(b) Trials of a new type of rear fuselage brake fitted to a Hunter with a production type jet pipe. The brakes were also to be fitted lower down the sides of the fuselage which, at worst, might prove whether or not the jet efflux was the cause of the trouble.

(c) Trial of the flap-type brakes using a slower operating mechanism so that the pilot could trim out the trim changes as they occurred.

In late January the interconnection flap with tailplane was finally abandoned, while in February 1954 the rear fuselage type was also abandoned.

On 6 February an under fuselage airbrake was flown with, in due course, very satisfactory results, and this was considered acceptable by Service pilots. However, to begin with it still did not produce adequate deceleration. A production version of this new airbrake was delivered to A&AEE for trials on 20 April and tests on the position under the fuselage forward of the wing were continued on WT566 during June 1954 with unsatisfactory results. In the end no fewer than twenty-one versions of airbrake were tried by Hawker before an acceptable one was devised.

In January 1956 Hawker began trials with double airbrakes to provide improved drag. These were carried out on XF379 and the conclusions drawn covering the air speed and Mach number range up to 600 knots (691mph/1,119km/h) and Mach 1.05 included the following:

1. The improvements in deceleration, especially at the high air speeds, were considerable and the additional drag was much appreciated compared with the 'standard' airbrakes. With the airbrakes fully open at 60 degrees, and power 'on', the deceleration time from the full throttle level speed of 520 knots (599mph/964km/h) IAS at 10,000ft (3,048m) to 360 knots (415mph/668km/h) IAS was 60 seconds. In comparison, with the single airbrake the speed had just stabilised at 415 knots (478mph/769km/h) IAS within the same time period. The increased drag was most marked in the first 20 seconds, the speeds falling to 425 knots (489mph/787km/h) IAS (double airbrake) and 470 knots (541mph/756km/h) IAS (single airbrake).

2. A progressively increasing but smooth nose up trim change was present. With airbrakes fully open this reached unacceptable proportions above 400 knots (461mph/742km/h) IAS but the effects decreased with reduction in airbrake angle.

3.   The buffet level was acceptable throughout the speed range at angles up to approximately 45 degrees. At angles in excess of 50 degrees the buffet increased proportionately with airspeed up to 450 knots (518mph/833km/h) IAS, above which speed it remained fairly constant.

A generally favourable impression of the double airbrake installation had been formed although it was considered that some development work would be necessary to reduce the nose up trim change and to lower the buffet level.

After tests with F.Mk.1 WT566, a production version of the under-fuselage airbrake was fitted to WT573. The initial trials found that the nose down pitch on extension and retraction at high Mach numbers and high IAS were of greater magnitude than had been experienced with the prototype airbrake. This was attributed to the fact that the operating times of the production version were much quicker and so caused the trim change to be more sudden. After a series of tests, with various modifications being tried, it was found that the gap between the airbrake leading edge and the fuselage when the airbrake was opening was very critical. Tests were made with the leading edge extended by various amounts and with different fairing shapes fitted to the fuselage. The most satisfactory arrangement was found with a convex-shaped fairing in place and the airbrakes opening to 60 degrees, and this arrangement was adopted for production aircraft. Later tests were made with the airbrake leading edge modified to blend with the fairing at all angles. This shape when coupled with a fairing of shorter chord and the airbrake opening at 67 degrees gave better characteristics, a reduction in the buffet level and approximately 10 per cent increase in effectiveness.

This fuselage side-mounted airbrake arrangement was tested by Armstrong Whitworth-built F.Mk.6 XF379 in 1956.

Early Mk.1 WT557, first flown on 17 July 1953, was photographed by Hawker photographer Cyril Peckham on the build-up to that year's Farnborough Show. (Phil Butler)

Another Mk.1 image from Hawker's photographer, WT594 in 1954.

The effectiveness of the F.Mk.1 Hunter's RAF camouflage scheme is demonstrated here by WT687. (Air-Britain via Phil Butler)

Increasing the F.Mk.6 extension from 60 degrees to 67 degrees also just about compensated the weight growth from the Mk.1 to Mk.6. The airbrake deceleration characteristics, previously criticised by A&AEE and CFE, were now thought by CFE to be fairly satisfactory in most operational conditions, but criticisms which remained were that the airbrake did not assist in reducing the height required for recovery from supersonic dives, and at speeds below 300 knots (345mph/556km/h) IAS (the limiting speed for flap) resort had to be made to flaps in controlled let downs to increase the drag. In fact the drag characteristics with the airbrake extended did not meet the standards considered desirable for an aircraft with a secondary ground attack role. The design of the brake was such that it retracted automatically on extension of the undercarriage because of the risk of fouling the ground, which meant that airbrake drag could not be used to improve the approach characteristics and shorten the landing run.

Tailplane

The saga of the Hunter tailplane is nicely summed up by test pilot Sqn Ldr R.N. 'Bob' Broad, who was the project officer for the CFE trial on the electric follow up tail (and who features again in Chapter 4). He says:

A serious criticism of the Hunter, particularly by ex-F-86 Sabre pilots, was that it didn't have a flying tail, but instead a powered elevator and an electrically operated tail plane trimmer. The elevator became ineffective at about 0.96 Mach, the air loads were such that it couldn't be moved, and further, any movement that could be made didn't have much effect. Recourse then had to be made to the tailplane trimmer which was effective. Hunter Mk.1s and early 4s (and I think all 2s and 5s) had a boosted elevator which did give a large and powerful pilot a slight edge. Later 4s and all 6s came in with a fully powered elevator where a hydraulic jack did the work and a spring provided the feel. This was slightly better in that every pilot could now get the maximum elevator movement but it had the snag of 'jack stalling' when the air loads on the elevator exceeded the power of the elevator jack (2,000lb/907kg) and the pilot came up against an apparent stop, which could be disconcerting. As always the elevator trimmer was used to give added control at high Mach numbers but this could cause problems. Late model Mk.6s introduced the electric follow up tail which automated the use of the elevator trimmer and was accompanied by a more powerful jack of 3,500lb (1,588kg), which was clearly much easier, safer and effectively produced a 'flying tail'.

Hawker Aircraft publicity views of a rocket-armed Hunter.

This sequence of photographs shows Hunter F.Mk.5 WN958 equipped with bombs or rockets together with drop tanks under the outer wing tanks.

In June 1953 Hawker's proposal for a simpler interim electrically operated flying tail was agreed by the MoS, in fact at the same time as a 'slab' tail was being developed. A 'slab' tail had first been proposed in January 1953 to deal with the inadequate effectiveness of the elevators and ailerons reported after flight testing of the second prototype. The MoS placed a contract for the development of a 'slab' tail in August 1954 but this was then cancelled in November 1956. The interim flying tail made its first flight on 23 January 1954, and in early April 1954 the Air Staff became worried about the operational limitations likely to be imposed on the Hunter through elevator ineffectiveness at high Mach numbers. The MoS was approached and stated that it had already asked Hawker to fit a flying tail, which at the time was basically an interlinked elevator/tailplane arrangement actuated by an electric motor. The actuator had proved unsatisfactory and was being replaced by a hydraulic jack. MoS clearance of the modifications to introduce a fully powered elevator to the F.Mks.1, 2, 4 and 5 was given in October 1955.

Hawker Dunsfold's testing of F.Mk.4 WT705 to assess the electric flying tail with 3,500lb (1,588kg) effort elevator booster (with light spring feel fitted) was performed by Neville Duke, Flt Lt A.W. 'Bill' Bedford and Hugh Merewether in almost 6 hours of flying over nine flights made between 9 September and 11 October 1955. Dives were initiated by pushing over from level flight at 0.91 IMN, 45,000ft (13,716m), and recovery action was taken when the IMN reached 1.05, which was usually at about 32,000ft (9,754m) in a 45 degrees dive. The maximum speed achieved in these flights was Mach 1.07. The results showed that the electric flying tail in its present form had markedly improved the Hunter's longitudinal gun platform stick manoeuvrability at high Mach number, and supersonically +4 to +5'g' (accelerometer reading) was now obtainable on the stick alone, compared to only +2'g' with the standard full powered elevator. A&AEE completed trials with the electric tail in February 1956 and recommended its fitting to all Hunters to improve their aiming and tracking at high speed and altitude, to increase manoeuvrability, and increase control in pull out from ground attacks. (The tailplane saga features again in Chapter 3.)

Tightening in Turns and Pitch-Up

In June 1954 A&AEE discovered that the Hunter, like the Swift, suffered from a tendency to tighten in turns although the characteristic was not so marked. However a 4'g' restriction was imposed on the aircraft. There was little hope of developing a simple modification to eliminate this pitch-up and after June 1954 the use of a fence was tried and discarded, and then an extended drooped outer wing leading edge was fitted in October 1954. In fact wing 'fences' proved unsuccessful in curing tightening and a tapered drooped leading edge was tried first. In January 1955 this proved to be unsuccessful and so the installation of a parallel drooped leading edge was begun. In October the parallel version was found by A&AEE to give considerable reduction in tightening in turns and the Establishment reported that the incorporation of the parallel leading edge extension modification resulted in a definite improvement in the pitch-up characteristics of the F.Mk.6. Pitch-up had been alleviated and the buffet and manoeuvre boundaries raised to an extent readily appreciable in mock combat. It was thus recommended that this should be fitted to all Hunters and particularly the Mk.6.

In late summer 1955 a total of 16 hours of flying was carried out by A&AEE on XF833, WW592 and XF376 to provide a general appraisal of the F.Mk.6, although only XF376 was a fully representative Mk.6. This was before the parallel drooped leading edge was ready, which is reflected in the statements that follow.

Due to the larger engine it had been necessary to re-introduce the rear fuselage tanks, which gave a CofG range similar to the F.Mk.1. However, the CofG movement with fuel consumption was different from the Mk.1 and resulted, during the middle part of a sortie, in the CofG being further aft than in any other Hunter. The Mk.6 also had the full power elevator and, although this had been adopted with enthusiasm on the Mks.4 and 5, it had not previously been fully assessed at extreme aft CofG positions.

The increased thrust from the RA.28 had resulted in high IAS and IMN being more readily available. In fact due to the increased thrust and weight it had been found that it was easier to reach 0.97 IMN than in the past and that the greater part of all flying at altitude was carried out at above 0.90 IMN, but the full power elevator offered only a slight improvement in control at these Mach numbers. It was impossible and undesirable to keep the Mach number down to speeds at which adequate longitudinal control was available and an interim flying tail was considered essential. Particular emphasis had been given to high IAS and it was considered that control with the full power elevator at an aft CofG was too sensitive. At 500 knots (576mph/926km/h) and above it was possible to apply high values of 'g' with a very small stick movement and force and it was found that higher 'g's were frequently applied than had been intended. The excessive longitudinal sensitivity also resulted in pilot induced overcontrolling and this resulted in severe porpoising. This overcontrolling was only likely to occur in bumpy conditions when out of trim due to airbrake extension or use of the tailplane at high IAS/IMN combinations. In fact the worst overcontrolling was experienced during a pull out at 576mph (926km/h) during which the airbrake was extended and the throttle closed.

Four manufacturer's views of F.Mk.6 WW593. This aircraft first flew on 19 August 1955 and was used by Hawker and A&AEE for various trials programmes. (Air-Britain via Phil Butler)

WW593 was eventually rebuilt as an FR.Mk.10.

The basic character of the F.Mk.6 pitch-up was similar to that of the Hunter F.Mk.1 due to the increased weight, but the pitch-up was more likely to occur in the Mk.6 and, due to several reasons, would present a greater danger and operational inconvenience:

1. The increased thrust boundary made it more likely that instability 'g' would be reached before the IMN had dropped.
2. The full power elevator meant that high values of 'g' could be applied more rapidly and easily, which made the resultant pitch-up more violent and increased the risk of pitch-ups at lower levels.
3. Due to increased weight the pitch-up would occur at a lower 'g' and there would be less chance of the IMN falling off.
4. Due to the sensitivity of the elevator at the aft CofG and the light stick forces, recovery from a pitch-up resulted in a violent nose-down pitch, which particularly applied to medium altitudes where the IAS was higher. It was instinctive for the pilot to put the stick fully forward when a pitch-up occurred.

Measured decelerations with the airbrake fully extended to 67 degrees had been carried out at 3,000ft (914m) and 580 knots (668mph/1,075km/h), and, with the throttle closed, it had taken 40 seconds for the aircraft to slow down to 300 knots (345mph/555km/h). This showed little deterioration on previous airbrake performance with the engine throttle, but the general impression to the pilot was that the airbrake was far less efficient; the buffet level was higher at all speeds and there was a residual nose up out of trim on extension. The residual nose up out of trim state after extension, coupled with the sensitivity of the elevator, had frequently resulted in pilot-induced porpoising at speeds above 500 knots (576mph/926km/h).

Gun Problems

The history of the Hunter's gun problems was spelled out in Ministry documents and essentially embraced three separate elements: airframe damage caused by spent gun ammunition cartridges and by gun blast, aircraft 'pitch-down' when gun firing, and the effects on the engine from gun gases. In general, all of these troubles stemmed from the unprecedented firepower of the new four x 30mm Aden gun installation (which had been developed and produced concurrently with this new aircraft) coupled with the introduction of high velocity ammunition.

As early as June 1951 the MoS had warned Hawker of the need to ensure that spent cartridges and links would be ejected well clear of the aircraft. Test firings on a Bristol Beaufighter fitted with the new weapon had resulted in damage to that aircraft's tail surfaces and for the Hunter the need was to prevent empty links striking the aircraft's structure and entering the air intakes. In February 1952 the Air Ministry enquired about progress with the spent link problem and was told that Hawker was 'facing it squarely', but in June, having failed to make the Aden guns fire properly in the course of seven months of ground trials, RAE took over the investigation. In November Hawker was asked to start immediate development of a spent link collection scheme or some alternative.

In March 1953 tests on the F.Mk.2 prototype showed links striking the airframe and in January 1954 Hawker was told that if satisfactory deflectors were not available then collector tanks must be fitted for gunnery trials at A&AEE. Two months later the firm stated that aircraft fitted with link chute extensions would soon be delivered for gun firing trials and that it had stopped work on collector tanks. However, A&AEE did not receive an aircraft for gunnery trials until May, the same month that the Air Ministry pressed the MoS to hasten gun firing at high altitude since the Americans were experiencing engine compressor stall when firing the guns on an F-86 Sabre. In June A&AEE found that gun firing on the Hunter was also producing damage to the nose structure, and in July that spent cases had caused damage to the airbrake.

In August A&AEE reported that deflector plates were not good enough to prevent spent links striking the aircraft and so trials of 'blister' tanks large enough to hold all of the links would be necessary. Later that month a Hunter's nose wheel door operating rod failed at Boscombe as a result of gun blast.

By March 1956 external link collectors had been produced which were being fitted to Fighter Command aircraft as part of a general modification programme. A modified gun pack in which links were to be fed back into the ammunition tank was on trial which, if accepted, would eliminate the need for external blisters, but in the end the famous twin 'Sabrina' containers fitted beneath the forward fuselage were introduced which stayed with the Hunter for the rest of its operational life.

Despite strengthening, there were further failures of the nose wheel rod, and nose wheel lowering failures associated with gun firing were still being experienced in April 1955. RAF gun firing trials in August 1955 continued to reveal damage to the nose structure and nose wheel mechanism. In truth the blast of the four Aden cannon was so powerful that it was causing damage to various components in the aircraft's nose, which occurred mostly as the result of firing at high speeds and low altitudes. The most serious effect was that the nose wheel door might become unlocked and in consequence the aircraft might tip on to its nose on landing and be damaged. However, as the Hunter's primary role was high altitude interception this trouble was operationally less serious than engine surge, but if it could not be cured then the secondary ground-attack role would be seriously jeopardised. Numerous modifications to strengthen the affected parts had to be devised and eventually an improved form of blast tube seal was introduced to prevent the escape of gun gases into the nose wheel area.

Next, when air firing, and particularly at high altitude, the aircraft suffered a marked pitch-down change of attitude which resulted in serious 'aim wander'. This was reported by A&AEE in June 1955. In August the establishment added that no appreciable change occurred in attitude when a single gun was fired, but there was a marked nose down pitch when all four guns were fired at once. Pending a solution to the problem, if necessary a great improvement could be achieved by temporarily restricting firing to just two guns, which would still give the Hunter greater firepower than the four x 20mm cannon that hitherto had been standard in the RAF and which was still in use in some types of US fighters.

Because the guns were disposed off the aircraft's centreline below the vertical position of the CofG, the kick from their firing induced a nose down pitch with a consequent effect on accuracy (a displacement of 1 degrees implied a miss by 50ft (15m) at 1,000 yards (914m)). This pitch-down effect had been predicted several years previously by MoS calculations and at first it was accepted by all concerned that it could be dealt with by pilot anticipation. Indeed, in January 1953 RAE calculated that in certain circumstances gun firing would produce a nose down pitch of 2½ degrees but this was not expected to be beyond the power of a pilot to anticipate. Later, when firing trials began, this particular problem was overlaid by the other gun firing troubles, which were considered to be of greater urgency. Eventually, however, the RAF expressed concern about the detrimental effect pitch-down would have on aiming at high altitude and Hawker began work on mechanical devices, which would counteract the violent kick from gun firing. In the end the firm developed a blast deflector that proved a substantial success.

Few gun firing trials on any Avon-powered Hunters had been undertaken by May 1954, when the Director of Operational Requirements became worried at the increase in compressor stalling with gun firing experienced by the Americans. Consequently, the Director of Operational Requirements asked the MoS to expedite trials on the Hunter 'to make certain we were in the clear'. Directly after this in June 1954 A&AEE reported engine surge was being experienced with gun firing at altitude.

In fact an investigation into engine surge, which first came to light on the Supermarine Swift, had already revealed that the Hunter Mk.1 suffered from the same defect. Symptoms had been noted by Hawker's pilots during early flying but these had not been identified as compressor surge. Arrangements were made by the Air Staff with the MoS for a Hunter to be made available to Rolls-Royce to undertake work to cure this defect and this aircraft (WT565) arrived at Rolls-Royce on 11 January 1954. In March the MoS reported that although modifications had been incorporated to overcome the surge, these had so far entailed derating the engine, which naturally affected the engine's operational capability. In September 1954 A&AEE experienced engine surge with the F.Mk.1 which was definitely attributable to gun firing at high altitude and low air speed – it had not been established previously whether the surge experienced during gun firing had been caused by, or was independent of, gun firing. Later the surge with Avon-powered aeroplanes was, with the right combination of flight factors, experienced under a variety of flight conditions. This was a highly undesirable phenomenon and was caused by the Avon's variable swirl-vane system. A method of fuel dipping (where the fuel flow was reduced briefly as the guns were fired) in due course eliminated the problem, but finding the cure took a long time.

The gun installation in the Hunter was a source of considerable trouble during the fighter's development programme.

F.Mk.1 WT570 and F.Mk.2 WN892 were used for high altitude firing trials between August 1954 and March 1955. The Avon 113 stalled regularly on firing low velocity (LV) ammunition at 40,000ft (12,192m) and above at low speeds in straight flight and under 'g' at higher speeds. The stall free altitude was therefore less than 40,000ft (12,192m), making the aircraft quite unsuitable for the high altitude interceptor role. Concurrent RAE tests showed that these characteristics were worse with high velocity (HV) ammunition. The Sapphire 101 in the Mk.2 was free from compressor stall below 48,000ft (14,630m) both with high and low velocity ammunition, and the stalls which were experienced at 48,000ft (14,630m) occurred in conditions not likely to be encountered in the tactical role and were also mild compared to those of the Mk.1. No 'flame-outs' were encountered and the F.Mk.2 was not, therefore, regarded as being restricted in the tactical role by compressor stall induced by firing the guns.

Experiments with this pair of aircraft – fitted with baffles and strakes (longitudinal fins) to deflect respectively the gun gases and pressure waves away from the air intake – were very successful using LV ammunition. Unfortunately, they did not prove effective when HV ammunition was employed. The modifications to be made subsequently to the Avon 115 which was to power the F.Mk.4 were known as Stage 2 modifications and were as follows:

(i).   A small increase in the size of the final nozzle, coupled with a slight increase in governed engine speed.

(ii).   Fuel and compressor bleedings during firing. The fuel was bled from the pilot burner manifold, and the compressor was bled at its final (12th) stage.

(iii).   Modifications to the engine to prevent nullification of the effects of the fuel and compressor bleedings.

(iv).   The introduction of a delaying relay into the electrical circuit of the guns.

(v).   An increase in the area of the turbine high pressure nozzle vanes, which in fact was an additional protection against surge in all conditions.

   In the event substantially improved surge conditions on the Avon 115 engines were experienced after they had been modified to this Mk.121 standard.

However, during firing all Hunter marks (both Avon and Sapphire) also experienced gas concentration in the gun pack and in March 1956 the firing limits were as follows:

A). F.Mks.1 and 4 (Avon):
Low velocity ammunition up to 35,000ft (10,668m) and 400 knots (461mph/742km/h) maximum speed.
High velocity ammunition up to 25,000ft (7,620m) and 250 knots (288mph/463km/h) maximum speed.
In addition the guns were not to be fired below 200 knots (230mph/370km/h) nor at a speed beyond the point at which buffet began when acceleration was applied.

B). F.Mks.2 and 5 (Sapphire):
Low velocity ammunition up to 48,000ft (14,630m) and 400 knots (461mph/742km/h) maximum speed.
High velocity up to 48,000ft (14,630m) and at 250 knots (288mph/463km/h) maximum speed below 25,000ft/7,620m and 350 knots (403mph/648km/h) above 25,000ft/7,620m.

For all marks the length of burst was not to exceed 1.5 seconds at 3 second intervals, although modifications were subsequently devised which permitted the firing of 2 second bursts at 4/5 second intervals and these did improve the still limited operational effectiveness of the Mks.1 and 4.

Surge-free conditions during gun firing were experienced with the F.Mk.6's Avon 201 engines. Testing of the Avon 121 eventually brought success as well and Hunters fitted with this engine were able to fire their guns without engine surge at the heights and speeds insisted upon by the Air Staff.

Reheat

Another element to disturb the Hunter's design and development was the installation of reheat (afterburning), and after Issue 2 of OR.228 had been released in January 1948 the facility was considered seriously to enable the new aircraft to meet the specification. When F.3/48 was issued in October 1948 it called for provision to be made for reheat on a scale to be agreed later but in October 1949, when it became evident that the first prototype would be ready for flight before the reheat installation was available, it was decided to fit non-reheat jet pipes with provision for a retrospective fitting. In December 1950 an assessment made by RAE indicated that the P.1067 with 1,500 degrees reheat could just meet the requirements of OR.228, but without it the aircraft would be down on level speed and fall short of the climb requirement by 60 per cent.

A meeting held on 21 February 1951 revealed that Hawker was experiencing great difficulty in fitting reheat and getting the CofG right and so, despite a final decision to continue to design and build the aircraft to take reheat, the firm was cleared to design an alternative rear end without it. In October Hawker decided to lengthen the aircraft's fuselage nose by 6in (15.24cm) to balance the reheat installation when it was installed, but by February 1952 the design team was doubtful that Rolls-Royce would have the reheat installation ready for the promised date of November 1952. A decision was therefore required as to which rear end should be fitted to production machines, otherwise production would be delayed, and this resulted in the move to have the first fifty examples without reheat. In January 1953 prototype WB188 was grounded for a preliminary installation of reheat to be fitted (which was given priority 'A' at a review of development items made on 25 February). Shortly afterwards, however, Hawker reported that it was having a great deal of trouble with the rear fuselage fuel tank and was endeavouring to introduce wing fuel tanks, and because of the difficulty over the CofG from the weight of the reheat installation the firm was proposing to delete the rear tank.

In an April 1953 Ministry list of Hunter problems still to be solved, by far the most important was the introduction of reheat to permit the fighter to achieve the specified performance requirements in full. Unfortunately, at this time not only had the basic development of engine reheat in the UK lagged behind schedule, but Rolls-Royce was also having great difficulty in fitting it into the Hunter. There was further delay and it looked like the installation would have to wait until the 101st production aircraft, not the 51st. By now the wing tank installation was also likely to be delayed owing to technical difficulties, which had necessitated a considerable degree of redesign. By September 1953 it was evident that, although reheat had now been fitted in WB188, the extent of the modifications on the production line to enable the facility to be installed; the provision of extra fuel; and the CofG problem; would create serious delays. It was therefore decided not to produce a reheat version but rather to install a Series 200 Avon which would provide increased thrust. The result was the F.Mk.6 and reheat was never again seriously considered for British Hunters, although in a project to improve the performance of the Mk.4s in Swedish Air

Prototype WB188 seen after modification with reheat as the Hunter Mk.3. Besides its record breaking achievements this aircraft was also used for trials with airbrakes on each side of the rear fuselage, for which the actuator fairing and brake hinges are visible alongside the rear fuselage serial number.

Force service (as the J34) several were in 1958 fitted with a Swedish-designed reheat installation. While this significantly increased the engine thrust, it provided little improvement in the fighter's performance and the project was eventually shelved.

The reader will have realised that many Hunters were used for testing and trials work, so to end this chapter it is worth recording the examples that formed part of the MoS Air Fleet by 20 August 1957. F.Mk.1s WT556, WT561, WT564 and WT573 were in temporary storage at 5 MU at Kemble and WT557 at 33 MU Lyneham and all were awaiting disposal; WT565 was under repair at Hawker Blackpool; and WT571 and WT656 were at RAE Bedford, the former also awaiting disposal. WT572 and WT621 were attached to the ETPS at Farnborough while WW605 was with RAE Farnborough. Six F.Mk.2s were listed – WB202 with Hunting Percival at Bedford; WN889 at Armstrong Siddeley at Bitteswell and WN891 at AWA at Baginton (both awaiting disposal); WN890 was at RAE Farnborough; WN892 with A&AEE Boscombe

and WN893 with RAE Bedford. The F.Mk.4 listing was WV375 at Hawker Dunsfold and WT703 at A&AEE, WT704 (5 MU Kemble), WT706 (RAE Farnborough) and XF994 (Rolls-Royce Hucknall) were all awaiting disposal; WT735 was also at RAE Farnborough and WT736 was attached to Ferranti at Turnhouse. The three F.Mk.5s reported were WP114 with Armstrong Siddeley at Bitteswell and WN954 and WN955 both at A&AEE.

There was a long list of F.Mk.6s. XK140, XG290 and XJ714 were at A&AEE; XF373 and XE558 were under repair at Hawker Blackpool; XF374, XF378, XE587 and XJ694 were at Hawker Dunsfold; XF375 was with Rolls-Royce Wymeswold; XF377 was under repair at Armstrong Whitworth at Bitteswell; XE588 and XE601 were at Hawker Kingston; WW592 at RAE Farnborough; P.1109 WW594 had joined CFE at West Raynham; P.1109 WW598 was with RRE Defford; and XF833 had joined Rolls-Royce at Hucknall. Finally, both T.Mk.7 prototypes XJ615 and XJ627 were listed as 'ex-development contract' but had not yet been accepted.

Formerly an F.Mk.6, XG168 was converted into an FR.Mk.10 in which form it is seen in this manufacturer's publicity photograph.

Recognition photos of the two-seat prototype XJ615.

During early 1955, with its gun firing and other problems, there was some public criticism of the Hunter. However, an extract from *Hansard* (the official report of proceedings for both the House of Commons and the House of Lords), dated 10 March, quoted a speech which was intended to try and quell the complaints. This declared that the Hunter was a first-class fighter which was flowing rapidly into squadron service. The need to incorporate certain modifications, such as the dive brakes, had delayed full operational clearance and there were still some restrictions on firing the guns. But the account clarified that these were largely due to the enormous four gun punch which had been packed into the aircraft to enable it to kill the enemy bomber. High combat speeds and nuclear bombs made this killing power enormously important and the Hunter could hit about nine times as hard as its predecessors. The report added that there was no doubt that the aircraft could deal effectively with any type of bomber likely to be available to attack the UK for some years, it was popular with its pilots and to say that the Hunter was anything but a success was wrong!

A comparison was also made between the Hunter and the Soviet Union's Mikoyan MiG-15 and MiG-17 fighters, noting that the Russians had produced fighters quickly at the expense of aids and firepower and had also sacrificed control characteristics at the high speeds of modern combat. These shortcomings had been amply demonstrated in Korea where MiG-15s had suffered severe losses at the hands of North American F-86 Sabres, and yet much was still being made in Britain of the MiG-15 and MiG-17. A proper comparison between the British and Soviet types really had to be made on the basis of their efficiency against bomber attacks. An interceptor fighter must have adequate performance, good flying qualities, powerful armament, and must form part of an efficient fighter defence organisation, and in these respects the report declared that the Hunter was certainly much better than the MiG-15 and indeed better than the MiG-17 as well.

CENTRAL FIGHTER ESTABLISHMENT

three

This chapter looks at the trials undertaken by the Central Fighter Establishment to help clear the Hunter for Service use. However, the approach here was different from that at A&AEE, concentrating as it did on the aircraft's tactical use and its capabilities against selected opponents. The text that follows does in places refer to some of the aspects covered by Chapter 2.

CFE Assessment

The Central Fighter Establishment or CFE, an organisation which belonged to the RAF, was a key facility in preparing fighter aircraft for the front line. Its objective was to test new fighters and their equipment, often against other fighter types and/or other aircraft; the development of fighter aircraft tactics; and to train squadron and flight commanders. Formed in 1944, CFE moved to West Raynham in October 1945 and would receive a number of Hunters for review. The identities of some of the examples to visit West Raynham for the trials outlined below has not been confirmed.

In September 1954 a report was issued describing tactical trials performed with the F.Mk.1, the main element being to assess the type's suitability to

Near plan view of F.Mk.6 XK151, which shows the extended outer leading edge very well. First flown on 16 June 1957 this was the last Hunter fighter issued to the RAF and it was later modified to FGA.Mk.9 standard. (Terry Panopalis)

WT626 was an F.Mk.1, which flew with No.229 Operational Conversion Unit but apparently never reached a front line squadron.

intercept and destroy bombers in general, and those operating at high speed and high altitude in particular. For aerobatics, CFE's pilots reported that the aircraft was light and responsive to the controls and all standard aerobatic manoeuvres could be performed with ease, although a considerable amount of height might be gained or lost during manoeuvres in the looping plane. Flick manoeuvres were not permitted. The fully powered ailerons made the Hunter a highly manoeuvrable aircraft at all altitudes. However, the elevator controls became heavy at high indicated airspeeds and ineffective at an Indicated Mach Number (IMN) of 0.96 by virtue of the stick forces required. Above this IMN initiation of manoeuvres in the longitudinal plane was limited by the rate of trim of the variable incidence (VI) tail.

It was thought that pilots unaccustomed to flying with powered controls would be surprised on their first take-off by the lightness of the stick forces required and the effectiveness of the controls, particularly the ailerons. Very high rates of roll were possible at high speeds and, in order that the ailerons were not overstressed under these conditions, the hydraulic jacks were designed to 'stall' within a safe aileron load. Flight in manual control showed that the controls were quite heavy even in the low speed range, and became progressively heavier as the speed increased. The main problem involved in flying in manual was the slow response to the controls owing to the stick forces necessary and the large air space required to complete manoeuvres. The controls were unbalanced at the low end of the speed range flown (120–500 knots / 138–576mph / 222–927km/h) IAS with the elevator being lighter than the ailerons.

During the final turn onto the target the IMN had to be kept to about 0.86 and below 0.96 in order to achieve the best results. Above 0.96 the elevator control was inadequate and resort to the tail trimmer had to be made. This was slow in operation and emphasised the shortcomings of the VI tail configuration. If the speed was allowed to drop by turning too tightly then the poor acceleration at low speeds at high altitudes made it necessary to dive several thousand feet in order to reach an IMN of 0.95 quickly, and so carry out a climbing attack onto the target. The best attacks were those resulting from a shallow dive onto the target at 0.96 IMN or less in the 10 to 15 degrees cone. The conventional quarter attack at 45,000ft (13,716m) was difficult to execute owing to the distance ahead of the target to which the fighter had to position and the problem of maintaining contact.

Aircraft which visited A&AEE Boscombe Down were often used to provide a series of photographs for recognition purposes. This series of Mk.1 WT687 is a case in point. (Air-Britain via Phil Butler)

Four Mk.1s took part in Exercise Dividend (an air defence exercise held in July 1954) and proved very satisfactory, clearly showing the marked superiority of this fighter over any other previously operated by the RAF. It was the first time the Hunter had appeared as part of Britain's air defence. The quick start achieved with the cartridge starter and rapid climb to altitude enabled targets flying at 45,000ft (13,716m) to be intercepted within 12 minutes of the scramble signal being given. The quick turns round achieved when using pressure refuelling were described as quite outstanding, and in one case four aircraft were turned around in 7 minutes using only three bowsers. The report noted that the Hunter Mk.1 had an effective radius of action of 200nm (370km), allowing for 10 minutes at full combat power at its operating height of 45,000ft (13,716m).

During this CFE trial numerous fighter versus fighter sorties were flown against the Sabre Mk.4 and by virtue of its better power/weight ratio the Hunter F.Mk.1 outperformed and outmanoeuvred this aircraft at all altitudes. However, the superior longitudinal control of the Sabre gave it a slight advantage in the initiation of manoeuvres. This was especially noticeable in the longitudinal plane and became more pronounced as the IMN increased. It was clear that the Hunter would benefit from the addition of a flying tail. In addition, in fighter versus fighter combat adequate rear vision was a vital factor and in this respect the Hunter was not considered fully adequate for the purpose, the Sabre being far superior.

Sorties were also flown against a Sabre Mk.5 made available by the Royal Canadian Air Force and powered by that country's 6,300lb (28.0kN) Orenda Mk.10 engine and the two types compared very closely. Details of their performance were as follows:

(a). Climb. The Hunter's climb was superior up to 30,000ft (9,144m) when the Sabre was 1,500ft (457m) below it. From this height the Sabre's rate of climb became very slightly the better and the Canadian fighter was only 600ft (183m) below the Hunter at 48,000ft (14,630m). The Sabre would continue to climb to 54,000ft (16,459m) when the Hunter's absolute ceiling was approximately 52,000ft (15,850m).

(b). Acceleration. On take off the Hunter accelerated appreciably faster than the Sabre. At altitudes the Hunter accelerated more quickly provided that the speed was kept above 0.85 IMN but below this speed there was very little difference, although the Sabre had a slightly better acceleration at speeds below 0.8 IMN.

(c). Turns at Altitude. Turning capabilities at altitudes over 40,000ft (12,192m) were very similar, but once the Hunter was forced to reduce speed to below 0.82 Mach it lost ground to the Sabre.

(d). Dives. Initially the Hunter would accelerate more quickly than the Sabre in a dive, but once an IMN of 0.95 to 0.97 was reached both aircraft were similar, unless the Sabre remained at 0.97 IMN when the induced drag due to wing drop would allow the Hunter to pass it. The Hunter would, however, reach a slightly higher IMN in steep dives.

(e). Manoeuvrability. Provided the speed was kept to above 0.85 IMN, the two aircraft compared very closely. The Sabre had an advantage in initiating manoeuvres with its superior longitudinal control at high IMN, at low altitudes the Hunter possessed a superior rate of roll at speeds in excess of about 345mph (556km/h) IAS.

It was clear from this comparison that fitting of the Orenda to the Sabre brought that aircraft, from the performance aspect, virtually into the Hunter Mk.1 class.

The report concluded that the Hunter F.Mk.1 was an excellent all round fighter which was suited to the interceptor role against the English Electric Canberra or the North American B-47 type of bomber. It had a considerable all round performance superiority over the Sabre Mk.4, but only a slight advantage over the Sabre Mk.5, and the Hunter also had a very considerable advantage over the rival Supermarine Swift F.Mk.1. The fully powered ailerons, and the VI tail with the boosted elevator, added to the stability of the aircraft, resulting in well balanced controls up to speeds of 0.96 IMN or 610mph (981km/h). The feel of the ailerons was not, however, fully satisfactory, and it was considered that there was some room for improvement.

In January 1955 CFE reported on a similar assessment of the Sapphire-powered F.Mk.2. On a scramble a climb on a straight vector to 45,000ft (13,716m) was achieved in under 9 minutes, covering between 68 and 73nm (126 and 135km). Employing full power at the top of the climb saw the acceleration to 0.94 IMN take under 1 minute, provided that it was commenced at the correct climbing IMN of 0.86 for this height. The report added that the F.Mk.2 was not well suited to the low level role because of the fuel that it carried. For aerobatics this version was the same as the F.Mk.1 and the recommended speeds were as follows – roll 350 knots (403mph/648km/h), loop 425 knots (489mph/787km/h), roll off loop 450 knots (518mph/833km/h) and upward roll 500 knots (576mph/927km/h).

CFE tested various Hunters in mock combat against the F-86 Sabre. Over 400 examples of
the Mk.4 with a General Electric engine were supplied by Canadair of Canada to the RAF.

Model of the Hawker P.1067 when it still featured a T-tail.
(George Cox)

Prototype WB188 pictured on display at the International Air Tattoo at Greenham Common in 1976. This aircraft had made its last flight in 1954.

Early photograph of WB188 possibly taken prior to its first flight.

Early views of Hawker Hunters in RAF service. (MoD)

Colour image of Fireflash Hunter XF310 seen landing at the September 1957 Farnborough Show. (Terry Panopalis)

During 1958 F.Mk.6 XF389 was used to demonstrate underwing rocket carriage. (Peter Green)

Hunter F.Mk.6 XG164, 'H' of No. 74 Squadron, was later converted by Armstrong Whitworth to FGA.Mk.9 standard. (MoD)

The prototype T.Mk.7 XJ615 is seen at Farnborough in September 1956.
(Adrian Balch)

T.Mk.8 trainer WW664 attended the SBAC Show at Farnborough in 1958. This aircraft was one of the F.Mk.4s converted to two-seat configuration. (Peter Green)

XL586 seen in RAF service in about 1959. This aircraft was built as a T.Mk.7 and carries the registration 'RS-90', denoting No.229 OCU (Operational Conversion Unit). (MoD)

An early F.Mk.5, powered by a Sapphire engine.

Manufacturer's view of the one-off two-seater G-APUX.

G-APUX attended the 1959 Farnborough Show. (Peter Green)

Another attendee at the 1959 SBAC Show was this rocket-armed single-seat Hunter.

The FR.Mk.10 prototype XG168 was displayed at Farnborough in 1960. (Peter Green)

Formerly a P.1109 Hunter, WW594 is pictured at St Athan in September 1965 after having been converted back to standard F.Mk.6 configuration.

XG210 was an F.Mk.6 which was used at times for research work and here the Hunter is pictured at RAE Farnborough in September 1966. (David Hedge)

WW598, the second Hawker P.1109A, in the splendid original blue and white colour scheme applied to the aircraft after it had completed its Firestreak role and joined RAE's test fleet in the 1960s. It is pictured at RAE Llanbedr. (The late Arthur Pearcy via Peter Green)

In 2001 GA.Mk.11 WV256 was repainted in duck-egg green to represent prototype WB188 in the form that it first flew in 1951. This was done as part of the celebrations to mark the 50th Anniversary of the Hunter's first flight and here the aircraft was photographed at the air show at Kemble held on 22 July 2001.

Prototype WB188 was used to test reheat for the Hunter airframe. After its retirement from flying this aircraft served as the gate guard at Melksham, where it is seen during the 1950s.

This F.Mk.4 WV325 was photographed almost certainly in late summer 1955 when it was flying as 'C' with the Central Flying School. (Mike Stroud)

Manufacturer's publicity picture of WB202.

The tip-tank Hunter XG131 pictured in flight on 5 October 1956. (Peter Green Collection)

XE610 pictured here in the late 1950s or 1960 as 'J' of 74 Squadron. By the end of 1960
work had begun on converting this aircraft into a Mk.9.

Having previously served with The Black Arrows aerobatic team (No. 111 Squadron), XF446 is seen in the late summer of 1966 after its conversion to FGA.Mk.9 and in the hands of 54 Squadron as 'B'.

It is likely that these ground shots show XG290, here loaded with two underwing bombs. The nose angle in particular presents a large amount of Hunter airframe detail.

The Hunter's rival in early days was the Supermarine Swift. This is WK205, a Swift F.Mk.1
photographed in mid-February 1954. (MoD)

Two Swifts from No. 79 Squadron are seen flying with two unidentified Hunters, the lower of which comes from No. 14 Squadron and the upper from No. 26 Squadron.

One other fighter to join the RAF at around the same time as the Hunter was the Gloster Javelin night fighter. During the second half of the 1950s the Hunter, Swift and Javelin represented the Service's new and modern front line. (Jet Age Museum)

Rare flying shot of XF833 after the thrust reverser had been fitted. Two black bands were painted around the fuselage for photo interpretation (the second is just behind the wing trailing edge). (Peter Green Collection)

Although the main intention at CFE was to assess the F.Mk.2's interception capability, again its ability in the fighter versus fighter role was tested with sorties against the Sabre Mk.5. Here during the take off and climb the Hunter Mk.2 accelerated away from the Sabre and continued to do so until 30,000ft (9,144m) when the latter started to reduce the advantage gained. At 30,000ft (9,144m) the Hunter was 6,000ft (1,829m) above the Sabre and at 50,000ft (15,240m) it was 2,300ft (701m) above. In level flight the acceleration at the 45,000ft (13,716m) and 35,000ft (10,668m) levels indicated that there was little difference in the acceleration characteristics of the two types up to 0.90 IMN. Above this speed the Hunter slowly started to gain an advantage and at the end of the 3 minute period of acceleration at 45,000ft (13,716m), when the two aircraft had reached near maximum speed, the Hunter was 300 yards (274m) ahead of the Sabre. At 35,000ft (10,668m), at the end of 2.5 minutes, the Hunter was 400 yards (366m) ahead and was opening the range at a slightly faster rate than that evidenced at 45,000ft (13,176m). In fact as the altitude was decreased the acceleration advantage of the Hunter Mk.2 increased correspondingly.

In turns and manoeuvres made in the looping plane at speeds in excess of 0.92 IMN the Sabre outperformed the Hunter at all altitudes, while the turning radii of both aircraft in level turns at speeds below 0.92 IMN were approximately equal at altitudes above 30,000ft (9,144m); below that height the Sabre's radii was slightly less. In addition the Hunter appeared to lose speed more rapidly than the Sabre when pulled into the high speed stall or buffet area, and there was no doubt that these results were due primarily to the inadequate longitudinal control and slight 'dig in' tendencies of the Hunter. In high speed dives the superior acceleration of the Hunter became more pronounced in dives of any angle. However, it was found that in steep dives in excess of Mach 1.0 any advantage gained in the dive was lost in the pull out because of the Sabre's superior longitudinal control. Full power shallow dives of 0.95 IMN proved to be the most effective method of utilising the Hunter's superior acceleration and higher speed. In terms of level speed, at sea level the Hunter was approximately 23mph (37km/h) faster than the Sabre, at 15,000ft to 20,000ft (4,572ft to 6,096m) this increased to 29mph (47km/h) and was then reduced gradually until at 45,000ft (13,716m) and above the speeds of both aircraft were almost identical.

Mock combats were performed between 20,000ft and 48,000ft (6,096m and 14,630m) and it was found with the Hunter attacking that the only manoeuvre the Sabre pilot could do which would assure him of not being fired upon was a high 'g' diving turn at speeds in excess of 0.90 IMN followed by a roll in the direction of the turn and a pull through. Recovery from the resulting dive was made with dive brakes extended and at maximum available 'g'. The Hunter pilot, while following through this manoeuvre, found that even using the VI tail trim to the maximum he did not have sufficient longitudinal control to bring his sights to bear upon the target. In the dive recovery he found himself well below and ahead of the target which placed the Sabre pilot in a position to make an attack. The Hunter then had to climb straight away at its best climb speed to prevent the Sabre from closing the range and making an attack.

With the Sabre attacking, the Hunter's only method of preventing the Sabre from getting into a firing position was a straight shallow dive to 0.94 IMN followed by a straight climb at the optimum climbing speed of 0.87 IMN or above, or by continuing the dive. All manoeuvres initiated by the elevator were neutralised by the very effective longitudinal control of the Sabre and the Hunter pilot was committed to level, climbing or very shallow diving turns, for when the speed exceeded 0.92 IMN the Sabre's superior longitudinal control became the deciding factor. This left the Hunter pilot committed to a straight climb until such time as adequate displacement could be made for a 180 degrees turn back towards the Sabre. The Hunter then had to be at least 3,000ft (914m) above and 3nm (5.6km) ahead to prevent the Sabre 5 from opening fire in this turn.

At low altitude, around 10,000ft (3,048m), it was found that with the Hunter attacking, the Sabre pilot could apply sufficient 'g' in turns to prevent the Hunter laying off deflection, and by making the plane of his turn intersect the horizon at approximately 30 degrees he could utilise his longitudinal control in such a manner as to gain in the turn on the Hunter. In addition, the Sabre pilot could pull his aircraft into the buffet without danger of pitch-up and loss of speed, whereas the Hunter pilot had to fly his aircraft so as not to enter the buffet area, for once in this zone the 'dig in' occurred with resultant loss of speed and control. With the Sabre attacking, the Hunter could pull 7.5'g' and yet the Sabre could maintain a lead angle throughout the turn. The Hunter could accelerate and climb away when the pilot deemed necessary, but if he tried to turn with the Sabre he was out-turned and the Sabre was able to get into a firing position.

The results of this phase of the trial showed that in all instances, if the Hunter tried to dog-fight the Sabre would end up behind the Hunter, and if the Hunter did not break off the engagement by climbing or accelerating away then the Sabre would eventually close the firing range. In conclusion the Hunter held the initiative in rate of climb, acceleration and speed and could therefore engage the Sabre or break off the combat at will, but this advantage became less pronounced as altitude increased. By virtue of its superior longitudinal control, however, the Sabre could outmanoeuvre the Hunter if it allowed itself to be drawn into a dogfight. This was particularly noticeable, and quite decisively in favour of the Sabre, at speeds in excess of 0.92 IMN – the Hunter was hopelessly outmanoeuvred at the higher speeds. This highlighted the importance of providing adequate longitudinal control for an aircraft throughout its entire speed range, and in particular at the higher speeds, and it was regretted that the Hunter F.Mk.2 did not possess this vitally important characteristic. However, the Mk.2 was an excellent fighter which was well suited as an interceptor of the bomber capable of a speed of 0.8 IMN at 45,000ft (13,716m). By virtue of its increased thrust and the excellent handling qualities of the Sapphire engine it had a considerable advantage over the Hunter F.Mk.1, and again it showed a very marked advantage over the Swift F.Mk.1.

Next to be tested by CFE were the F.Mks.4 and 5 which underwent tactical trials as interceptors in July 1955. Mk.4s WE744 and WE746 and Mk.5s WE985 and WE991 were delivered to the establishment on 26 April 1955 and, using the same parameters as for the Mks.1 and 2, the trial was completed on 30 June. It was found that their changes in fuel loads, and thus all-up-weights

and the further forward CofG which resulted from them, had had a slightly detrimental effect on the performance of the Mks.4 and 5, but this was declared acceptable in view of the greater range and endurance now available to both versions.

The acceleration after take off was rapid and in the climb both the Mks.4 and 5 were basically stable and little or no change of trim was required until a height of 25,000ft (7,620m) was reached. From there to 45,000ft (13,716m) the trim changed gradually from 1 degrees nose down to 0 degrees nose down. Even with their additional internal fuel both marks were still not well suited to the low level interceptor role. At 390 knots (449mph/723km/h) IAS at sea level the F.Mk.4 had a maximum range of 325nm (602km) but a combat radius of action of only 56nm (104km), allowing 10 minutes' combat time, while the range of the F.Mk.5 at sea level was 345nm (639km) and its combat radius 47nm (87km).

The instructions for turning onto a target were the same as those given for the Mk.1 above and the report noted that it was quite impossible to carry out an attack of any description while in manual control. Indeed, an immediate withdrawal from combat had to be made and, if operating over enemy

Gloster Aircraft photographer Russell Adams took this splendid series of images of Mk.4 WV319, which retains the original Hawker Hunter wing leading edge. WV319 was later converted to T.Mk.8 standard. (Jet Age Museum)

Another Mk.4 to be photographed by Russell Adams was WV325 in 1955.

territory or where enemy fighters were particularly active, the Hunter pilot would find it impossible to defend himself if he was suddenly attacked while in manual control. For fighter versus fighter combat both the Mk.4 and Mk.5 exhibited longitudinal control (so important a factor in air fighting) which was poorer than that of the Mks.1 and 2 due to their increased weight and more forward CofG, and which in fact left much to be desired. It was clear that with their present longitudinal control it was not possible to derive from these aircraft the full performance of which they were capable either in an attack on bomber aircraft or in fighter combat, and which was of prime importance in air combat throughout the speed range.

The report did add that the Mks.4 and 5 were still well suited to intercept the bomber capable of a speed of Mach 0.8 at 45,000ft (13,716m). The tendency to pitch-up of the Mks.4 and 5 was less pronounced, and easier to control,

than that of the Mks.1 and 2 but there was no doubt that the Hunter would be a better fighter if this feature could be eliminated. Finally, the fully powered ailerons and the VI tail with a boosted elevator combined to produce well balanced controls up to a speed of 0.9 IMN, but above this speed longitudinal control became progressively less effective, until at 0.96 IMN it could only be achieved by the slow operating VI tail trimmer.

In October 1956 the Air Fighting Development Unit (AFDU) within CFE reported on tactical trials with the F.Mk.6. The greater all-up-weight of 17,600lb (7,983kg) over earlier marks was more than compensated for by the increased thrust of the RA.28 (200 Series) engine and had resulted in an improvement in performance with a shorter take-off run, shorter time to height, faster acceleration and deceleration, and a slight increase in maximum level speed. The acceleration from 0.7 to 0.92 IMN at 1,000ft (305m) for example took 22 seconds while the Mk.4 took 42 seconds and the Mk.5 28 seconds; at 40,000ft (12,192m) the respective figures were 77, 105 and 100 seconds. The engine handling characteristics were better, although the increased fuel consumption resulted in a considerably reduced radius of action and ferry range, making it even less suited to the high speed, low altitude, interceptor role than the Mks.4 and 5. At 484mph (778km/h) IAS at 1,000ft (305m) the Mk.6 had a range of 256nm (474km) but a combat radius of action of only 60nm (111km), allowing 5 minutes for combat at full power and the same landing reserve. With two pylon drop tanks the figures at 1,000ft (305m) were increased to 420nm (778km) and 137nm (254km).

All climbs were made at full throttle with full internal fuel and ammunition. The maximum indicated altitude recorded on initial climb was 52,500ft (16,002m) and at this height, which took approximately 17 minutes to attain, the rate of climb had dropped to nil. The F.Mk.6 took 12 minutes 20 seconds to reach 50,000ft (15,240m) while the F.Mks.1, 2, 4 and 5 took over 16 minutes, 12 minutes 30 seconds, 18 minutes and 17 minutes 30 seconds respectively. In general the manoeuvrability of the Mk.6 was approximately the same as that of the Mk.4 with the fully powered elevator below 40,000ft (12,192m), and slightly better above that height, where the increased available thrust had a proportionately greater effect on the manoeuvre boundary. In a turn initiated at 0.9 IMN and with full throttle used throughout, no height being

lost during the turn and the speed kept constant, the Mk.6 showed a lower radius of turn than the Mks.4 and 5, 2.7nm (5.0km) against 2.9nm (5.4km) at 40,000ft (12,192m) and 5.0nm (9.3km) instead of 7.6nm (14.1km) at 48,000ft (14,630m).

At high IAS flight the fully powered elevator, the stick movement and therefore the force per 'g' became progressively smaller as the IAS was increased, and at 576mph (926km/h) and above it was easy to over-control and allow the aircraft to porpoise, particularly in turbulent conditions and when the airbrake was open. Below 0.93 IMN the F.Mk.6 was pleasant to fly, highly manoeuvrable and an effective fighting aircraft. Above this speed, however, air loads on the tail were such as to stall the elevator jacks; longitudinal control could then only be achieved by resorting to the VI tail trim, which was too slow in operation to be of any practical use for tracking a target or evading a pursuer. For example, below 45,000ft (13,716m) it became easy to exceed 0.95 IMN during a diving attack and the report emphasised again that the Hunter could not be used to its full advantage until it was fitted with a control column actuated tailplane. (At the time it was understood that all Mk.6s were to be fitted eventually with an electric follow up tail which would give the same control effectiveness as a direct hydraulic control column actuated tail, only with a slight delay.) The pitch-up characteristics of the Mk.6 did not differ appreciably from those of the previous marks, and in fighter versus fighter

  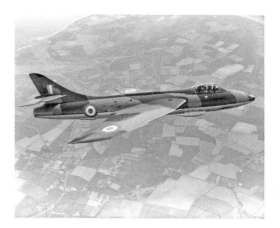

A further batch of manufacturer's publicity photos, this time showing off F.Mk.6 XE588 in 1957. First flown on 6 April 1956, this aircraft was used to perform Hunter demonstrations in Switzerland and then for spinning trials, during which the aircraft was lost in a crash on 9 November 1957. (Terry Panopalis)

XF389 was a Mk.6 built by Armstrong Whitworth and is shown here armed with rocket projectiles and without wing leading edge extensions.

combat the Mk.6 acquitted itself well provided the speed was kept below 0.93 IMN. The F.Mk.6 could intercept a bomber capable of 0.85 IMN at 45,000ft (13,716m) and its improved time-to-height gave an advantage over the Mks.4 and 5 – the Mk.6 could intercept 24 miles (39km) further out from base.

This report was followed in September 1957 with an account of tactical trials with a Hunter F.Mk.6 fitted with parallel leading edge extensions to the outboard section of the wing. Two aircraft were employed on the trial, XE628 in the modified form and XE608 unmodified, and the trials stretched from 18 to 31 July and embraced fifty-three flights over 35 hours 20 minutes flying time. In full power climbs to 48,000ft (14,630m) XE628 took 10 minutes 52 seconds to get to this height and the unmodified XE608 10 minutes 40 seconds. In level flight at 40,000ft (12,192m) with the aircraft positioned side by side and flying at 0.70 IMN, when full power was applied the two aircraft stayed in line abreast and accelerated to 0.945 IMN in 1 minute and 30 seconds.

To compare their combat capability nine sorties were flown with both aircraft together and after each flight the pilots were changed to counteract differences in pilot technique; eleven flights were also made with the modified aircraft in which it was engaged in air-to-air combat with formations from the Day Fighter Leaders Squadron. The longitudinal control characteristics were basically unchanged in the modified aircraft while a direct comparison at 40,000ft (12,192m) between the two aeroplanes showed that the leading edge extensions delayed the onset of buffet by approximately 0.2'g'. However, there was no apparent increase in useable 'g' at high altitude owing to the rapid onset of severe buffet in XE628, and the maximum 'g' available at high altitude did not appear to differ between the two aircraft. At medium altitudes (i.e. 30,000ft/9,144m or below) the modified Hunter had an advantage over the unmodified aircraft and could turn inside it until the unmodified aircraft pitched-up or stalled. The severity of the buffet in a hard turn with XE628 was a disadvantage, but the lateral rocking was reduced in comparison with XE608 during identical turns. The improvement in manoeuvrability continued to ground level, but in ground attack the limiting factor was normally the structural limitations and no alterations in tactical handling in ground attack were necessary. Nevertheless, in the ground attack role the delay in the onset of buffet was expected to provide a safety margin during a pull out for a misjudged attack.

It was concluded that above 30,000ft (9,144m) the capability of the F.Mk.6 in the interceptor role was not affected by the addition of parallel extended leading edges and in fighter versus fighter combat the modification provided increased manoeuvrability, while the old problem of pitch-up tendency had been markedly reduced which made for more precise control at high incidence.

This then new F.Mk.6, XK151 with the saw-tooth leading edge and belonging to the Central Fighter Establishment, was photographed being flown by Flt Lt K.J. Goodwin AFC, who over the previous two years had performed more than twenty Hunter demonstrations across Europe.

The stalling characteristics were also improved but the possibility of inadvertent spinning had been increased.

Three months later, in December, CFE reported on trials with the Hunter F.Mk.6 now fitted with an electric flying tail, 3,500lb (1,588kg) elevator boosters and the extended leading edges. Serial XK149, XK150 and XK151 joined CFE on 23 September, 30 September and 17 October 1957 respectively and trials flying began on 2 October. In all seventy-two flights were made totalling 45 hours 10 minutes' flying time. Basically, the modification consisted of an electrical interconnection of the tailplane and the elevator so that, on moving the stick, both elevator and the tailplane were deflected. The pitch-up characteristics of the aircraft fitted with the leading edges remained unchanged by the introduction of the electric flying tail, and no difficulty was experienced during this trial in recovering from inadvertent spins.

Compared with an unmodified Hunter, the aircraft was undoubtedly easier to control in the transonic region and the effect of the electric flying tail and larger elevator jack was twofold. Firstly, the larger elevator deflections available without 'jack-stalling' enabled a manoeuvre to be initiated with less difficulty and, secondly, the added effect of the tailplane following up nullified to some extent the lack of actual effectiveness of the elevator at high Mach numbers. Although a turn could be initiated more quickly, the sustained rate of turn remained unchanged. In comparative transonic dives, it was found possible to recover an unmodified Hunter in approximately the same height by full use of the tailplane trimmer, but this was not a suitable method of control at these speeds since overtrimming could and frequently did result. The electric tail on the other hand provided positive control with a single stick movement without risk of overtrimming. The take off was also noticeably more pleasant which was attributed to the combination of lighter stick forces and greater effectiveness. Overall, there was a distinct improvement in longitudinal control at high Mach numbers (although the longitudinal control above 0.97 IMN was still inadequate) and the safety margin during high speed, low level attacks had been increased. There was also an increased possibility of overstressing the aircraft at low altitude at high IAS.

In July 1957 F.Mk.6 XE608 (without wing leading edge extensions) was used as a comparison aircraft to XE628 (which had the extensions) in trials to assess the effects this alteration had on the new mark's performance. Here XE608 is pictured later in its career with extensions to the outer wing leading edge now in place.

In October 1957 XK150 was used by CFE to assess the F.Mk.6's electric flying tail. After an upgrade to FGA.Mk.9 standard, during the early 1960s this aircraft served with No.8 Squadron as 'A'.

Finally, six standard Mk.6s were assessed by CFE in the ground attack rocket firing role, the resulting report being issued in January 1958. The carriage of any external stores moved the CofG aft and in this configuration the aircraft was, therefore, slightly tail heavy. Nevertheless, the variant was found to be a very satisfactory and a stable rocket firing platform, and it was concluded that it was an aircraft that was easily and quickly modified for ground attack operations.

This text takes the Hunter development story up to the late 1950s when most of the clearance testing for UK service had been done. There was still some research and development work to do, much of it for overseas service as the orders for examples for other air arms began to roll in, but by this time the Hawker Hunter's biggest troubles were over and the aircraft had established itself as a true thoroughbred aeroplane.

Service Career – A Brief Review

To end this chapter a brief review of the Hunter's service career would seem appropriate to allow readers to get an idea of what followed the test programmes outlined above. The first RAF squadron to begin operating the Hunter, in July and August 1954, was No.43 and another thirty-six fully equipped squadrons and a host of support units operated examples in the UK, RAF Germany and with the service in the Middle and Far East. Seven Royal Navy squadrons also flew the type. Famous display teams were formed by Nos 92 ('The Blue Diamonds') and 111 'Treble One' ('The Black Arrows') Squadrons, and overseas the Hunter was used extensively by another twenty countries. The biggest operators included Belgium, Chile, Denmark, India, Holland (six squadrons), Sweden (four squadrons) and Switzerland (sixteen

Hunters in service. This picture, almost certainly taken at Jever in Germany, shows F.Mk.1s in RAF hands with WW655 closest to the camera.

squadrons and units and another famous display team – the Patrouille Suisse). Smaller air arms as far apart as Abu Dhabi, Kenya, Lebanon, Peru, Rhodesia and Singapore received examples, as did a few civilian organisations.

With its air defence and ground attack roles it was inevitable that the Hunter would become involved in conflicts. For the RAF they took part in operations in the 1956 Suez Crisis, and in Kuwait (1961), Indonesia (early/mid 1960s) and Aden (mid 1960s), although not all of these involved the use of weaponry. Dutch aircraft were present in Indonesia in 1962, but the first full-scale conflict to involve the Hunter was the Indo-Pakistani War in 1965. Indian aircraft also saw action in Assam in 1968 and a second conflict with Pakistan broke out in 1971. In 1966 Jordanian Hunters fought against Israeli aircraft, and during the Six-Day War with Israel in 1967 Jordan's Hunter fleet was totally destroyed. The 1973 Arab–Israeli conflict came next, in 1975 Omani aircraft bombed rebels on the South Yemen border, during the mid to late 1970s Rhodesian (Zimbabwe) aircraft attacked targets in Zambia, in 1983 Lebanese aircraft attacked forces in the Chouf mountains, and the Iran–Iraq War of the early 1980s saw further examples performing combat missions.

In conclusion the Hunter was not supersonic on the level but in a dive it could pass through the 'sound barrier' with ease. It was manoeuvrable, could absorb rough handling and in general was very much liked by its pilots. Today's aircraft enthusiasts are very lucky to have so many examples still flying (some of which continue to provide training for aircrew), a by-product of such a long and successful career.

Apart from its long service career the Hawker Hunter will always be remembered for its display abilities, both in solo and in formation aerobatics. Not least was the famous occasion at the 1958 Farnborough Air Show when No.111 Squadron's Black Arrows display team executed a world record loop of twenty-two aircraft.

TEST and TRIALS AIRFRAMES

A longside the prototype and production work described in the earlier chapters the Hunter was used for a good number of trials programmes, in some cases for new engines or missile weaponry or to test a new feature on the airframe, and a selection of these are described below. This list is by no means complete but it does embrace several of the most interesting projects and it makes use of files found at the Brooklands Museum, the National Archives and the Rolls-Royce Heritage Trust.

Area-Ruled Fuselage

In the summer and autumn of 1955 the RAE at Farnborough performed a series of tests on a Hawker Hunter to determine what reduction in drag could be achieved on the aircraft by fitting a fairing to the rear fuselage. This feature was designed to control the shockwave movements in the wing body junction and so reduce the transonic drag rise. This was entirely an RAE project and, apart from the modification work required on one Hunter airframe, it did not involve Hawker Aircraft at all.

By the mid-1950s many tests on wind tunnel and free flight models had shown that substantial reductions could be made in the transonic drag rise of conventional swept-winged aeroplanes by making suitable modifications to the body shape. Explanations and design methods had been offered in the area rule concepts propounded by Richard T. Whitcomb and Robert T. Jones in America, while ideas concerning shockwave control had been put forward by Dietrich Küchemann and John A. Bagley at Farnborough. The largest gains would of course be obtained by designing an aircraft from the

Publicity photo of Hawker P.1109 XF378 taken in 1957. (Peter Green Collection)

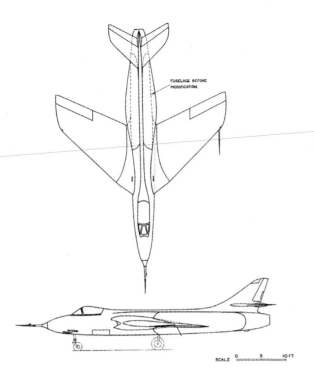

Above: Three-view drawing of Hawker Hunter F.Mk.1 WT571 fitted with the rear fuselage fairing. (Brooklands Museum)

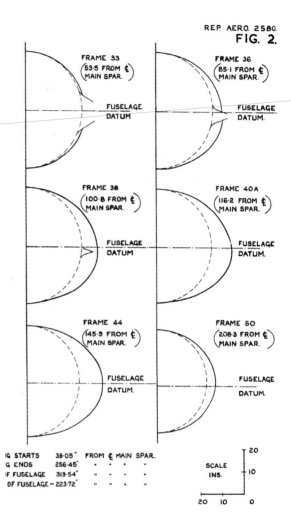

REP. AERO. 2580.
FIG. 2.

Above: Cross-sections taken through the rear fuselage fairing. (Brooklands Museum)

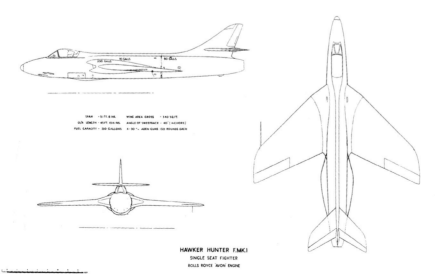

HAWKER HUNTER F.MK.1
SINGLE SEAT FIGHTER
ROLLS ROYCE 'AVON' ENGINE

Left: Hawker also put together a three-view drawing of an 'area ruled' F.Mk.1. (Brooklands Museum)

Front and rear views of WT571 taken at Farnborough after the aircraft had received the fairing on each side of its rear fuselage. Note the test probe on the nose.

Further close up view of WT571's modified rear fuselage. (Barry Jones)

outset to incorporate any necessary 'waisting' of the fuselage, but even on existing aircraft types it was thought possible that their drag could be reduced appreciably by the addition of suitable fairings.

In July 1954 John Bagley, an aerodynamicist at RAE, made some proposals for modifying the rear fuselage shape of a Hawker Hunter. However, because of the restrictions to the regions where changes could be made to the Hunter's fuselage, it was found that the fuselage fairings required to make the aircraft fully conform to the area rule theory would be very extreme in shape. Consequently, it was decided to use the Küchemann design method to determine the shape of the rear fuselage fairing, which meant that the resulting fuselage was not actually 'area ruled' but it did offer a potential increase in critical Mach number and a reduction in drag rise. The fairing produced by this method was found to be of an acceptable size and it would also conform to 'the mean area distribution requirements at a low supersonic Mach number' (in other words the fairing represented a partial fulfilment of the requirements of area rule at Mach 1.08). It was accordingly decided to fit this fairing to a Hunter to see if or what reduction in drag could be achieved.

The aircraft selected was F.Mk.1 WT571 which had first flown on 8 January 1954 and previously been used by RAE to measure the fighter's drag and to perform other research at Mach numbers up to 1.2. The static and pitot pressure errors of WT571 in its original F.Mk.1 form had been measured thoroughly and were used for the modified aeroplane after brief check measurements showed that the rear fairing had not altered the static pressure error of the nose boom system. WT571 had flown to RAE for the first time, from Dunsfold, on 1 April 1954 and it then returned to Dunsfold on 24 January 1955 for the modifications to be incorporated under Contract 6/Aircraft/11368/CB.5(b). On the completion of the work WT571 went back to Farnborough on 1 July 1955 and the flight test programme commenced soon afterwards.

When the trial was finished the Hawker diaries for October 1955 reported that the results of area rule tests on a 'modified Hunter' (i.e. WT571) indicated that the benefits were only very slight. Indeed RAE's final report, written by Messrs D.R. Andrews, F.W. Dee and D. Waters, was not in fact completed until November 1956, which perhaps reflected the lack of any major benefits provided by the fairing. However, a comparison of the results before and after modification showed that the fairing had delayed the onset of the transonic drag rise by about 0.015 in Mach number and the magnitude of the rise itself had been reduced. Beyond Mach 1.0 this gain decreased progressively – at 1.0 it had fallen to about 0.007 and it disappeared entirely at Mach 1.17. Beyond Mach 1.17 it appeared that the fairing might actually be increasing the drag of the basic aircraft, but RAE noted that these gains had been achieved for no

The standard 'slim' rear fuselage of the Hunter F.Mk.1 as displayed by WT565. Also visible
is the standard Hawker Hunter wing trailing edge.

increase in the subsonic drag and for no change in the handling characteristics of the fighter.

Indeed, the modification to the rear fuselage was found to have a negligible effect on the handling characteristics of the aircraft throughout the whole speed and Mach number range. A brief formation check with another Hunter indicated that the rear fairing had improved the maximum level speed performance by about 0.01 to 0.015 in Mach number, and a comparison between full throttle levels made before and after modification tended to confirm this improvement. The report declared that such an improvement in speed was to be expected from the delay in the onset of the drag rise already noted. However, the new fairing was never to be fitted to any other Hunter airframe.

In its modified form the basic data for WT571 was given as follows: wing span 33ft 8in (10.26m), wing area 340sq.ft (31.62sq.m), sweepback at ¼ chord 40 degrees, maximum thickness/chord ratio (symmetrical) 8.5 per cent, total fuel 334gal (1,519lit) and all-up-weight at take off 15,808lb (7,171kg). The engine was an Avon RA.21/113 giving 7,600lb (33.8kN) of thrust. On completion of its 'area rule' programme WT571 went to the National Aeronautical Establishment (NAE) at Bedford on 6 December 1955, before being released from its duties on 4 July 1957. It is unknown if the rear fuselage fairings were removed during its later flying career. On 22 September 1958 WT571 was despatched to RAE Farnborough to be used for fatigue testing work, and the aircraft was finally Struck Off Charge on 19 December 1959 and scrapped.

Supersonic Flap Blowing

Between 24 June and 20 September 1955 Hawker test pilots Sqn Ldr A.W. 'Bill' Bedford and Hugh Merewether flew F.Mk.1 WT656 on behalf of RAE to make an assessment of the Attinello Blown Flaps that had been fitted to the aircraft. This Hunter had first flown on 14 October 1954 and the system

View showing WT656 with the Attinello flaps raised. (Terry Panopalis)

that had now been installed had provision for selecting one-third, two-thirds or full blow; a long nose pitot with a swivelling head was used to serve the air speed indicator. WT656 was powered by a single Rolls-Royce Avon 113/5 (RA.7 Stage 2) engine and the take-off weight was 15,595lb (7,074kg), which included 2,672lb (1,212kg) (334 gallons/1,519 litres) of fuel. The design limitations on the airframe were +7.5'g' acceleration up to 585 knots (674mph/1,084km/h) IAS and/or Mach 0.94, and +6.0'g' acceleration up to 620 knots (714mph/1,149km/h) IAS and/or Mach 1.0. The flight test programme embraced general handling, measurements of lift coefficient and incidence, measured take offs, blown landing, stalls and position error measurements.

The aircraft had been fitted with this special form of boundary layer control (BLC), which enabled the wing to develop increased lift at low airspeeds, primarily for the purpose of reducing take off and landing speeds and distances. The BLC took the form of supersonic blowing over the special plain flaps, which were fitted in place of the Hunter's usual split trailing edge flaps. Air was bled from the 12th stage of the Avon compressor and was ducted to the wings where it was ejected at supersonic speed through a slot 0.060in (1.52mm) wide, which extended over the entire flap span. This slot directed the air along the top surface of the wing tangential to the flap nose where, due to an aerodynamic phenomenon known as the 'Coanda Effect', the jet would cling to the upper surface of the flap, following it round and down at whatever angle the flap was set. The efficiency of the device in maintaining unseparated flow over the flap was a direct function of the difference of speed between the jet and the mainstream air. Hence the maximum effectiveness of supersonic blowing air would occur under conditions of high engine rpm (revolutions per minute) (giving high duct pressures and temperatures) in combination with low aircraft speeds.

In this scheme the bleed air from engine compressor was controlled by two independent valves. One valve controlled approximately two-thirds of the total possible bleed and the other controlled the remaining one-third bleed. These valves were mounted on the engine and were electrically actuated (in fact the one-third bleed valve was the valve which was permanently on the Avon to regulate the engine anti-icing airflow). They were selected by a pair of ON/OFF switches mounted on the port cockpit shelf and each switch controlled its appropriate valve and corresponding proportion of the total bleed. Selection of both switches together would give full bleed and the valves took approximately 8–10 seconds to open fully after selection of the switches. The airflow was divided to port and starboard flaps after it had passed through the valves, so that a valve failure could not create any asymmetric blow.

Two images showing WT656 with its flaps lowered. (Barry Jones)

Flap operation was controlled by the normal flap selection lever mounted on the port instrument panel. The eight notches on the quadrant gave, successively, flap angles of 20 degrees, 35 degrees, 42.5 degrees, 50 degrees and 57.5 degrees, and then the last three notches all gave the maximum flap angle of 65 degrees. The flap was stressed for use as an airbrake and an angle of 65 degrees could be maintained to a speed of approximately 320 knots (368mph/592km/h) IAS, the flap blowing back at speeds greater than this figure.

Due to a rise of JPT when air was bled from the engine compressor, the jet pipe in this aircraft had been fitted with an enlarged final nozzle (20.15in [51.18cm] diameter as compared with 10.4in (26.42cm) diameter on the standard version). With no bleed this reduced the JPT at maximum rpm under sea level static conditions from 685°C to approximately 620°C, the thrust being reduced from 7,600lb (33.8kN) to an estimated 7,000lb (31.1kN). Thus, due to the necessity for a larger final nozzle, this aircraft (WT656) had approximately 8 per cent less thrust than a standard Hunter F.Mk.1 throughout its flight range. With full bleed turned on at maximum rpm, sea level static conditions, the JPT would rise from 620°C back to approximately 685°C, but a further loss of engine thrust of approximately 300lb (1.3kN) would be experienced. The results were as follows:

1. General Handling
a) Without Flaps.
The aircraft was flown up to 1.05 Mach number indicated and 550 knots (633mph/1,018km/h) IAS and the handling characteristics throughout this speed range appeared to be identical to those of a standard Hunter with flap retracted.

b) With Flaps.
The flaps (without blow) were operated in stages at speeds varying from 120 knots (138mph/222km/h) IAS up to 300 knots (345mph/555km/h) IAS at 10,000ft (3,048m). A much stronger than normal nose down trim change was experienced on extension of the flap through the first 20 degrees, such that full nose up tailplane setting and a pull force of some 3–5lb (1.4–2.3kg) were required to fly within the speed range 120–215 knots (138–248mph/222–399km/h) IAS. Further extension of the flaps to 65 degrees did not appreciably increase this nose down trim change and care was necessary to anticipate these nose down effects, particularly with increase in IAS above 200 knots (230mph/370km/h). Conversely, on retraction of the last 20 degrees of flap a marked unacceptable nose up pitch occurred such that at, for example 230 knots (265mph/426km/h) IAS, the tailplane angle to trim had to be changed

from 1.5 degrees nose up to 1.5 degrees nose down. The flap drag was considerably less than with the standard flap.

In addition to the trim change, the flap produced a beneficial nose down attitude, which increased with flap angle and with increase in ASI. At flap angles of 35 degrees or above moderate buffet was present increasing to a maximum with the flaps fully down at 65 degrees, a feature not normally experienced on standard Hunters.

c) With Flaps and Blow.
On selecting full blow at 150 knots (173mph/278km/h) IAS with flap down, a delay of some 10 seconds occurred after which a general but progressive increase in buffeting occurred, followed by a considerable nose down change in attitude and a slight nose down trim change. A 'ballooning' feeling was experienced as blow was switched on and the aircraft initially climbed some 100ft (30.5m) before settling down in a steady attitude. On increasing speed in a dive to 215 knots (248mph/399km/h) IAS it was noted that the buffeting increased proportionately with speed, reaching moderate but acceptable proportions. Small amplitude lateral and directional irregular oscillations were also present, the effects increasing with the buffet but never becoming marked. A light pull force and full nose up trim were required to fly at 215 knots (248mph/399km/h) IAS with full flap selected. Decrease in speed below 150 knots (173mph/278km/h) IAS resulted in a considerable decrease in buffet.

Switching to blow 'off' was possible under all conditions without any adverse effects, and subsequently during the take-off tests it was normal practice to cancel blow immediately after undercarriage retraction. The flaps, however, were always raised and lowered with caution in anticipation of the strong trim change. Operation of the blown flaps when flying in manual on the ailerons slightly improved the lateral control response and effectiveness, but made negligible difference to the forces.

2. Take Offs.
A number of measured take offs were carried out both with and without flap and with and without blow. The following was the general technique and a summary of the characteristics experienced during these take offs.

The aircraft was lined up on the runway and the engine was opened up to maximum power (8,000rpm) against the brakes. For the majority of take offs full nose up tailplane setting was used, although this involved considerable care after take off in anticipating the marked nose up effect present on retraction of the flaps. Full up elevator was applied to raise the nose wheel, the stick afterwards being held almost fully aft unless the aircraft showed a tendency to nose up quickly. In this case (which was usually only present on take off *without* flap) the stick was eased forward sufficiently to avoid 'unsticking' with an excessive attitude. Take offs were made with 0 degrees, 35 degrees and 50 degrees of flap, both with and without blow. The use of flap produced a marked nose down effect which caused an apparent decrease in tailplane and elevator effectiveness, resulting in a delay both in the raising of the nose wheel and in the aircraft's subsequent ground departure. The addition of blow slightly increased the basic nose down trim change of the flaps but appeared to make little difference to the actual take-off distance. Although no measurements were made, the distance from 'wheels rolling' to 50ft (15.2m) altitude appeared to be improved with blow 'on'.

After a flapped take off, with increase in speed a marked nose down attitude was present. On retracting the undercarriage at 200 knots (230mph/370km/h) IAS, the aircraft was in trim with full nose up tailplane setting. At 230 knots (265mph/426km/h) IAS, switching off blow at 500ft (152m) produced only a slight nose up trim change, but the retraction of the last 20 degrees of flap involved a marked unacceptable nose up trim change requiring a strong push force to hold, and subsequent retrimming from 1.5 degrees nose up to 1.5 degrees nose down. Take-off distances and runway winds were measured by ground observers.

3. Blown Landings.

A simulated landing was investigated at 10,000ft (3,048m). The aircraft was flown in level flight with wheels and flaps fully down at 125 knots (144mph/232km/h) IAS, 7,500rpm at a fuel state of 280gal (1,273lit) remaining. Full nose up tailplane setting, together with a 10–15lb (4.5–6.8kg) pull force, was required to fly at this condition. A medium amount of buffet was present with the flaps fully down and minor irregular lateral and directional oscillations were noted. The stick was eased back and speed was further reduced to 110 knots (127mph/204km/h) IAS at which conditions the aircraft became sloppy directionally and commenced a sluggish descent.

A brief landing investigation was carried out with blow operative and the following behaviour was typical. The aircraft was flown on the final approach at 7,000rpm and 130 knots (150mph/241km/h) IAS with wheels and flaps down, and blow fully on. At a fuel state of 180gal (818lit) remaining, full nose up tailplane setting, together with a pull force of some 15lb (6.8kg), was required to fly at 130 knots (150mph/241km/h) IAS. The lack of flap drag (due to a combination of the restricted flap angle of 65 degrees, together with the drag increase with blow) was most apparent on the approach and it

was felt that full advantage of the system was difficult to utilise for this reason and because of the high rpm necessary to provide a reasonable amount of blow. In addition the undulating approach path, together with not being able to trim out the nose down effect from the flaps, made maintenance of a low approach speed and steady angle of approach somewhat difficult to achieve. Just prior to crossing the runway threshold speed was decreased to 120 knots (138mph/222km/h) IAS by reducing rpm to 6,500 and the aircraft was allowed to sink down to the ground at 110 knots (127mph/204km/h) IAS. On closing the throttle the residual thrust was slow in dying away and had a slightly adverse effect on the landing distance.

The brief tests indicated that little benefit if any was present with this blown flap system in use for landing.

4. Stalls

Stalls were carried out at medium altitude at varying flap settings without 'blow' and at idling rpm. In the 'clean' condition the stall occurred at 102–110 knots (117–127mph/188–204km/h) IAS with the port wing dropping as the aircraft nosed up. With 35 degrees and no 'blow' the aircraft stalled rather abruptly at 102 knots (117mph/188km/h) IAS, nosing up and dropping the port wing quickly. At 50 degrees and no 'blow' the stall occurred at 101–103 knots (116–119mph/187–191km/h) IAS with the aircraft nosing up slightly and yawing to port, dropping the port wing fairly quickly through some 60 degrees of bank. Finally, with 65 degrees flap and no 'blow' the aircraft stalled at 100 knots (115mph/185km/h) IAS, nosing up and quickly dropping its port wing through some 45 degrees.

In Conclusion:

1. The aircraft had now completed a total of 22.35 hours flying covering take off, landing, stalling, measurements of position error and lift coefficient and incidence.

2. Although analysis of the results indicated a reduction in stalling speed of between 1 and 10 knots (1.2–11.5mph/1.9–18.5km/h), depending on the flap angle and engine rpm, full advantage of the blown flap system as applied to the Hunter could not be realised for the following reasons:

    a). The new flaps produced a strong nose down pitch which caused an apparent decrease in the elevator/tailplane effectiveness at low speed resulting in a delay both in the raising of the nose wheel and the aircraft's subsequent ground departure.

    b). Appreciable out of trim forces were present with flap down even when using full nose up tailplane setting.

c). The addition of blow slightly increased the nose down pitch but appeared to make little if any reduction to the take-off distance.

d). Although cancelling blow after take off was not in any way embarrassing, retraction of the last 20 degrees of flap produced a marked unacceptable nose up pitch, requiring a change of some 3 degrees in tailplane angle to trim.

e). The reduction of drag on landing present with the new flaps (due to the reduced flap angle of 65 degrees, combined with the drag increase present with blow operative) restricted the practicable engine speeds on the approach to 6,500–7,000rpm, with a consequent reduction in blowing effectiveness.

3. The only practical benefit from this blow flap system as fitted on the Hawker Hunter appeared to be the nose down attitude which improved the pilot's forward and downward view from the cockpit.

4. Additional adverse features were:

a). The basic reduction in engine thrust from 7,600lb to 7,000lb (33.8kN to 31.1kN) without blow, and still further to 6,700lb (29.8kN) with blow. (Note: It was understood when this report was written that a proportion of this extra 300lb (1.3kN) thrust loss with blow might be regained at the blowing slots.)

b). The extra weight of 96lb (44kg) involved in fitting the system.

5. The engine behaviour and general functioning of the flap blow system had been most reliable.

6. The addition of a tail parachute for the approach and landing appeared to be desirable, thereby increasing the aircraft's basic drag and allowing the use of higher rpm with associated increased benefits from blow.

Some notes: The concept of flap blowing was formulated and designed by John Salvatore Attinello, an aeronautical engineer who died in July 2000 aged 79. Over the course of his career Attinello worked with the National Advisory Committee for Aeronautics (NACA) and Fairchild Aircraft. One problem of using flaps on aircraft was that when they dropped down turbulence would be created on the upper side of the flaps, which caused airflow to break away and reduce the efficiency of the flap, thereby causing a loss in lift. BLC compensated for this by bleeding some air from the engine compressor out to where the flaps and the wings were joined and then to blow it as pressurised air over the flaps. This had the result of 'smoothing' out the turbulent air thereby re-establishing the efficiency of the flap. The Lockheed F-104 Starfighter was one of the first aircraft in the world to use the blown flap method or BLC developed by Attinello although, working in conjunction with the Grumman company in America, Attinello had first applied flap blowing in 1954 to a Grumman F9F-4 Panther jet fighter. Here, the trials revealed that the Panther's take-off speed was reduced by 20 knots (23mph/37km/h) while it was possible to increase its under-wing load by 3,000lb (1,361kg).

By 1955 sucking and blowing air over the flaps had become a well-known method of increasing the lift of a wing at low speeds. The first application of blowing to a British aircraft came when Vickers-Supermarine applied it to the Type 525 heavy fighter prototype, the company calling the technique 'supercirculation' – again compressor air was blown over the upper surface of the flaps when they were extended to prevent the break-away of the airflow. In the event, however, this system was not adopted for production Hawker Hunters, primarily as a result of the trials undertaken with WT656.

WT656 had made its maiden flight on 14 October 1954 flown by Hugh Merewether. On 16 November it was handed over at Dunsfold to have the flap blowing system fitted, and after the conclusion of the Hawker Aircraft trials described above it went to RAE Farnborough on 9 December 1955. A move to RAE Bedford followed on 28 April 1956 before the aircraft was released on 15 October 1957. On 6 December 1957 it began some barrier trials and on 3 December 1959 the aircraft went to Larkhill for noise tests at the rocket-firing site. WT656 was Struck Off Charge as scrap on 8 August 1960.

Fireflash Missile Carrier

One Hunter was specially adapted to carry two examples of the Fairey Fireflash beam-riding guided missile. Issue 2 of Specification F.3/48 of 23 March 1951 had stated that, besides its cannon, the Hunter should be armed with an air-to-air rocket battery and, ultimately, the Blue Sky missile, as the Fireflash was then called. However, the Fireflash version was also produced with a view to exports. Basically still an F.Mk.4 airframe, serial XF310 was fitted out to have the missiles suspended from the inner pylon stations on a spigot at the front and a ball and socket bearer well aft under the wing, picking up the tail of the weapon. This rear mounting also incorporated the missile's electrical connections while XF310's nose was lengthened, and the black dielectric nose cap radome enlarged, to accommodate the larger beam-laying Mk.2 ranging radar. The four-gun armament was retained although the camera port just aft of the radome was deeper and longer, and normal pitot heads were mounted at both wing tips.

The plan to convert an aircraft was reported to Hawker in early January 1956 and XF310 made its maiden flight with two missiles and the modified nose shape in place on 18 July. The aircraft's handling characteristics proved satisfactory and it was delivered to Fairey Aviation for missile trials on the 20th. It is understood that a Fireflash round was fired in flight soon afterwards. For that year's Farnborough Show the Hunter was painted blue underneath and carried no national markings, despite having a British serial number, while the two Fireflash were painted in a rather lurid colour. The project was run in co-operation with Fairey and successful firing trials were subsequently performed in North Wales. These were completed in January 1957 after which the aircraft was returned to Hawker, and in April it was agreed by Hawker and Fairey to produce a short descriptive brochure in order to stimulate interest in the aircraft/weapon combination. By the time of the 1957 show the dielectric nose cap had been exchanged for one of the original camera noses made for the FR.Mk.10 Hunter variant which had a vertical glass window but no camera.

The Fireflash programme did not progress beyond the development stage and XF310, having been declared surplus to requirements, was sold back to Hawker and subsequently converted to a T.Mk.7. As such it made another first flight on 24 April 1959 and today the airframe still survives in a museum in Australia.

Original Fairey photograph of the Fireflash Hunter XF310.

Armed with two rounds of the Fairey Fireflash beam-riding air-to-air missile and fitted with a modified nose for the missile guidance equipment, F.Mk.4 XF310 made its maiden flight in this form on 18 July 1956.

XF310 comes in to land in 1956.

Fairey Aviation publicity view of XF310 now with the FR.Mk.10 nose. Note the complete absence of any RAF markings, due to the fact that at this stage the Service did not want any insignia shown because it had not endorsed the weapon.

Side angle photo of XF310 with RAF roundels now in place.

Three Hawker publicity photos of the Fireflash-armed aircraft, here with the Hawker Siddeley Group logo painted on the nose. Fireflash was originally codenamed Blue Sky.

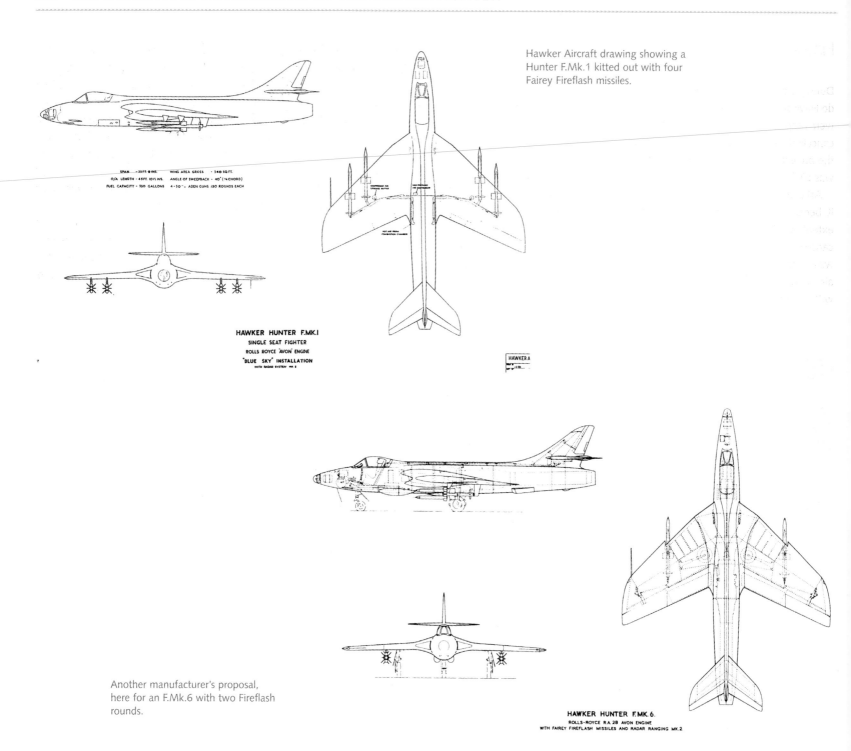

Hawker Aircraft drawing showing a Hunter F.Mk.1 kitted out with four Fairey Fireflash missiles.

Another manufacturer's proposal, here for an F.Mk.6 with two Fireflash rounds.

Hawker P.1109

During the first half of the 1950s there were studies to equip the Hunter with the de Havilland Blue Jay (Firestreak) air-to-air missile. Projects for a Blue Jay Hunter were prepared by the Hawker design team from 1953 but the work was officially cancelled by the Ministry on 28 May 1956. Specification F.167D was allotted to the project but was not proceeded with. However, in mid-June Hawker Aircraft was given permission to continue its Blue Jay work as a private venture.

After the cancellation of the Supermarine Swift jet fighter in the mid-1950s it became the Air Staff's intention to improve the Hunter to its maximum extent within a suitable timescale. With this in view, and because the Swift's cancellation necessitated a larger order for Hunters, the Ministry of Supply was asked to investigate the possibility of equipping Hawker's aircraft with air interception (AI) radar and de Havilland Blue Jay missiles (in conjunction with other developments such as increased engine power, etc.). This policy

was not to be confused with, or taken as a reversal of, a previous policy which had cancelled the supersonic P.1083 Hunter development (Appendix 1), an aircraft with thinner wings, more wing sweep, bigger engines, etc., that was abandoned because it offered inferior performance to the forthcoming supersonic English Electric P.1 fighter which became the Lightning. With increased engine power the radar/missile combination could be fitted to the standard subsonic Hunter without degradation of performance, and therefore would provide the type with increased capabilities (especially at night) and improve the deterrent value of the Hunter force in isolation. Hawker was asked to do a study and the firm called the new version the P.1109.

Estimates made in early February 1956 with the P.1109 fitted with a more pointed nose and an 11,250lb (50.0kN) thrust Rolls-Royce RA.24 Avon against a standard F.Mk.6 with the 10,000lb (44.4kN) RA.28/Avon 203 showed the following potential improvements in performance. The Mk.6's maximum level speed at sea level was Mach 0.94, and at 35,000ft (10,668m) Mach 0.96. For

After completing much of its manufacturer's flight testing, prototype Hunter WB202 was kitted out with four dummy de Havilland Blue Jay (Firestreak) air-to-air missiles. Flight trials were held between 21 May and 29 June 1954 and possibly into the following month as well. These were not connected with the later P.1109 programme but the Hawker diaries do indicate that the handling with WB202 with four missiles was 'very satisfactory'. (Peter Green Collection)

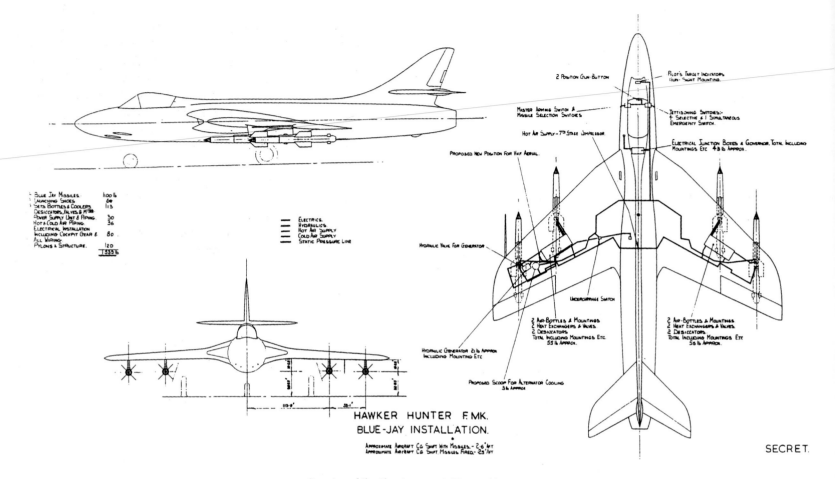

HAWKER HUNTER F. MK.
BLUE-JAY INSTALLATION.

SECRET.

Drawing of the Blue Jay-armed (Firestreak) Hunter.

the P.1109 the quoted figures were Mach 0.95 and 0.965 respectively when not carrying missiles, and Mach 0.945 and 0.96 with two Blue Jays aboard. Time from a standing start to 50,000ft (15,240m) was 11.90 minutes for the '6', and 8.80 and 10.80 minutes for the P.1109 without and with missiles, while the respective 1.5'g' ceilings were 45,400ft, 48,200ft and 46,100ft (13,838m, 14,691m and 14,051m) and radius of action for a combat sortie 322, 303 and 265 miles (518km, 488km and 426km). The respective take-off weights were 17,600lb, 17,200lb and 18,200lb (7,983kg, 7,802kg and 8,256kg).

The increased engine thrust would compensate for the additional drag from the missiles, while each P.1109 would carry only two guns to reduce the nose weight when the Mk.6 had four. The 'battle camera' was mounted on a protruding fairing on top of the nose (instead of being recessed in a trough as on standard Hunters) but, apart from the much-enlarged dielectric nose, the aircraft was largely standard. The P.1109s had no dog tooth on the wing leading edge and the external modifications to the nose shape – the most visible change – increased the aircraft's length by about 3ft (0.91m). In fact the standard Hunter nose was not visible to the pilot from the cockpit but the extended nose was clearly visible, and in flight gave a positive indication of any yawing or pitching motion, which might otherwise have passed unnoticed by the pilot. The view down from the nose was, however, also somewhat reduced.

In spite of the official cancellation of Hunter/Blue Jay development in May 1956, a letter dated 15 June 1956 was subsequently received by Hawker chief designer Sydney Camm from J.E. Serby, Director General of Guided Weapons (DGGW) at the Ministry of Supply, encouraging the firm to proceed with this project on a private basis. At this point work on converting some Hunter airframes to take the missile and/or its equipment and radar was already well underway. Hawker decided to proceed with brief trials and by August it had been agreed that the firm would equip and fly one aircraft fitted with Blue Jay missiles within a programme using three airframes. The firm would clear the handling aspects only before de Havilland Propellers (the weapon manufacturer) took the aircraft over for a limited programme of ground and air firing and dummy runs. There would be no attempt to clear the aircraft as a weapon system (when it entered service in 1957 Blue Jay was renamed Firestreak).

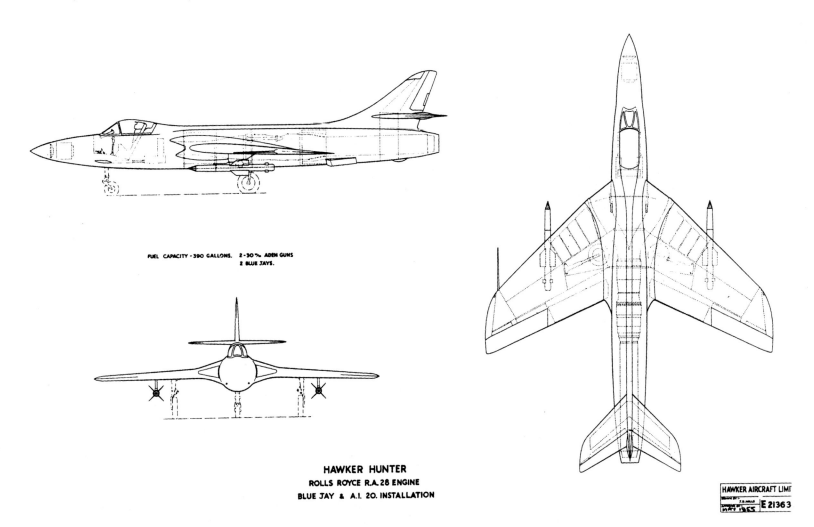

FUEL CAPACITY - 390 GALLONS.   2 -30 ⁷⁄ₘ ADEN GUNS
2 BLUE JAYS.

HAWKER HUNTER
ROLLS ROYCE R.A. 28 ENGINE
BLUE JAY & A.I. 20. INSTALLATION

HAWKER AIRCRAFT LIMI
E 21363

Hawker drawing from May 1955 showing the original P.1109 configuration. The engine was a Rolls-Royce Avon RA.28 and a total of 390gal (1,773lit) of fuel was to be carried, the same as a standard F.Mk.6.

Three F.Mk.6s, WW594, WW598 and XF378, were chosen for conversion to the new configuration, but only the last of these was completed as a fully equipped aircraft. Actually WW594 and WW598 proved to be more than aerodynamic test beds since they had the required AI.20 radar installed and a certain amount of Firestreak circuitry, but XF378 received the full Firestreak plumbing and pylons to carry the missiles. WW594 first flew on 23 September 1955, and on 7 December it was handed over at Hawker's Dunsfold airfield to be converted to P.1109A standard (which was the designation given to the aerodynamic test aircraft without missiles). On 16 May 1956 it was despatched to Defford to have AI.20 installed and to permit development trials to proceed. WW598 first flew on 31 December 1955 and soon afterwards joined the RAE Farnborough and Bedford High Speed Flight. It was converted into a P.1109A aerodynamic test aircraft in 1956 having been handed over on 19 January under Contract 6/Aircraft/11975/CB.9(b). XF378 was a Hunter built

Original Hawker photos of the first P.1109A WW594. (Phil Butler)

Nose angle view of the P.1109B XF378.

Hawker P.1109B XF378 pictured just after the modified nose had been fitted but prior to repainting.

by Armstrong Whitworth at Coventry and was despatched to Dunsfold from its Baginton birthplace on 26 September 1955 in readiness to serve as an AI.20 test-bed. XF378 was first flown with two Blue Jays and an AI.20 nose radar installation on 12 September 1956. On 24 October it was loaned for Blue Jay firing trials at RAF Valley and on December was used for a trial installation of a revised powered flying control system. In September 1957 the aircraft was loaned to Hawker so that it could appear at the SBAC Show.

The Green Willow AI.Mk.20 X-band fire control radar designed for single-seat fighters was manufactured only in a short run; in fact possibly no more than five examples. It was developed as a back up for the Ferranti AI.Mk.23 then being designed for the English Electric P.1 fighter, and which was experiencing some early problems, and a contract to begin AI.20 development was placed by the Telecommunications Research Establishment (TRE) in late 1953 (during 1953 TRE became the Radar Research Establishment or RRE). By 1955 flight trials were underway from RAF Defford, and as a ranging radar with a beam-riding capability AI.20 was installed in an Armstrong Whitworth NF.Mk.11 Meteor night fighter used for early Fairey Fireflash missile trials. Apparently the AI.20 system 'performed impeccably' (although pilot Bob Broad does not agree – see below), but its development was halted when AI.23 began to come through. Little or no data has been published in regard to AI.20's performance, but it is understood that at range of 7 miles (11km) there was 'a 95 per cent probability of a lock-on of a Hunter-size aircraft'. AI.20 was never used operationally – the examples completed were built purely for test and experimental purposes.

Two Hawker Aircraft flight test reports provide details of the relatively few differences experienced between the F.Mk.6 Hunter and the P.1109s. To begin with, between 21 March and 15 May 1956 WW594 was flown eighteen times by Hawker test pilots Sqn Ldr Neville Duke, Bill Bedford and Hugh Merewether. The aircraft was powered by an Avon 203 (the standard Mk.6 engine – the RA.24 was never installed) and the take-off weight was 16,810lb (7,625kg). Fuel load was 392gal (1,782lit) and the radar was not fitted, with 150lb (68kg) of ballast being used instead, the object being to clear the aircraft to its normal limits and note any effect that the altered nose shape might have on the handling qualities. The highest achieved airspeed was 620 knots (714mph/1,149km/h) and highest altitude 55,000ft (16,764m); the maximum recorded Mach number was 1.16. The aircraft was cleared separately to each of these figures and to 7.5'g' (the design limitation).

Initially the increased airflow through the cockpit to cater for the extra radar cooling proved to be an embarrassment, and trying for the pilot's eyes, and had to be reduced. A timed combat climb was carried out from wheels rolling with the result that 20,000ft (6,096m) was reached in 2 minutes 53 seconds

and 50,000ft (15,240m) in 10 minutes 47 seconds. Hugh Merewether then zoom climbed WW594 from an altitude of 52,000ft (15,850m) up to 55,000ft (16,764m) at 140 knots (161mph/259km/h), officially considered to be the highest altitude ever attained by any Hunter, and he found the aircraft's behaviour to be normal. During the climb the general handling was normal as were the Dutch rolling characteristics at altitude if the aircraft was laterally disturbed. However, the presence of the extended nose made any oscillations more noticeable than usual.

Several transonic dives were also carried out, the maximum Indicated Mach Number (IMN) of 1.16 being reached in a steep dive from 51,000ft (15,545m). Again the behaviour was normal for a Hunter, particularly with regard to any lateral or longitudinal oscillation. However, transonic dead rudder movement in the region Mach 0.95 to 0.965 IMN was noticeably more apparent than usual both on dive initiation and recovery. The aircraft was also flown up to its limiting airspeed of 620 knots (714mph/1,149km/h) and again the behaviour was found to be normal, even in turbulent air, but dead rudder movement was again apparent at Mach 0.94 to 0.95. The stall behaviour at 25,000ft (7,620m) was also typical of that displayed by F.Mk.6 Hunters – a directional breakaway to starboard commenced at 115 knots (132mph/212km/h) and the resulting wing low effect could not be held below 111 knots (128mph/206km/h) without suppressing the sideslip. Overall, the general handling of the P.1109A did not appear to have been appreciably affected by the altered nose but the characteristic dead rudder movement was now more noticeable than usual.

In September 1956 XF378, the P.1109B, which again was powered by an Avon 203, was checked out by Hugh Merewether and Duncan Simpson in four flights lasting just over 2.5 hours, and with two Blue Jays aboard the aircraft was cleared to 50,000ft (15,240m), 615 knots (708mph/1,139km/h), Mach 1.09 Indicated and 7.5'g'. To begin with, on 7 September XF378 was flown clean with the two inboard pylons empty at an all-up-weight of 17,026lb (7,723kg). It took 12 minutes 5 seconds to reach 50,000ft (15,240m) and there was a slight amount of lateral rocking towards the end of the climb due to poor aileron feel, which was heavy. The aircraft was flown satisfactorily to 620 knots (714mph/1,149km/h).

The aircraft was then flown with two uncharged Blue Jays on the inboard pylons on both 12 and 14 September and in this condition the aircraft's all-up-weight was 17,656lb (8,009kg). The nose wheel was raised at 105 knots (121mph/195km/h) with full up elevator and zero tailplane setting and the aircraft was comfortably airborne at 135 knots (155mph/249km/h) without the use of flap. Two combat climbs were carried out and respectively

The full P.1109B configuration with Firestreaks and AI.20 radar was represented by XF378, seen here without the missiles aboard.

Air-to-air publicity views of a fully armed XF378 taken in 1957. (Peter Green)

20,000ft (6,096m) was reached in 3 minutes 7 seconds and 3 minutes 10 seconds, and 50,000ft (15,240m) took 12 minutes 33 seconds and 12 minutes 55 seconds. In the climb there appeared to be a slight deterioration in lateral damping with the missiles fitted. A dive made from 48,000ft (14,630m) down to 25,000ft (7,620m) enabled the aircraft to reach Mach 1.09 – full nose down trim was required. With undercarriage and flaps down the stall was very gentle indeed and not accompanied by any lateral or directional change of trim. Full throttle level speeds at low altitude were recorded, with figures of 570 knots (656mph/1,056km/h) IAS at 5,000ft (1,524m) and 605 knots (697mph/1,121km/h) IAS at 2,000ft (610m).

It was of course important to fly the aircraft with only one Blue Jay aboard (in this case on the port side) to check the asymmetric handling after firing one missile. Here, on a second flight made on 14 September the take-off weight was 17,340lb (7,865kg). The aircraft took off and climbed away satisfactorily, an estimated maximum of one-third aileron control being required at the instant of unstuck to hold the aircraft level. The aircraft was dived to 1.06 IMN in power and there was a slight wing low tendency, but this was considered to be no worse than what could occur on some clean aircraft. When flown with ailerons in manual at about 20,000ft (6,096m) and 450 knots (518mph/833km/h) Mach 0.94 IMN full starboard tab was required for trimming, while at 0.95 IMN there was a heavy left wing low tendency, which could only just be held. With undercarriage and flaps down, full starboard tab plus a moderate single-handed force to starboard was required at 130 knots (150mph/241km/h) on the approach.

In conclusion, the general handling of the P.1109B XF378 with two Blue Jays fitted was very satisfactory and no adverse features were noted. Transonic handling was unaffected by carrying the missiles and the longitudinal trim appeared adequate for all flight conditions, but at 45,000ft (13,716m) the aircraft was just statically stable throughout its useable speed range. The aircraft could be landed single handed in manual ailerons with one missile retained.

In due course two Blue Jay missiles were satisfactorily fired from XF378 by de Havilland at the beginning of November 1956 and film of the air launch showed this to be the steadiest yet achieved on any installation of this weapon on any aircraft. XF378 also attended the SBAC Show at Farnborough in the first week of September 1957, the first time that the P.1109 configuration had been shown to the public, and the lack of further entries in the Hawker diaries for the P.1109 makes it sound as if the Blue Jay trials programme was pretty well done and dusted by the time of Farnborough. However, the three airframes did find other roles as related below, and there was to be another brief study for a Firestreak Hunter.

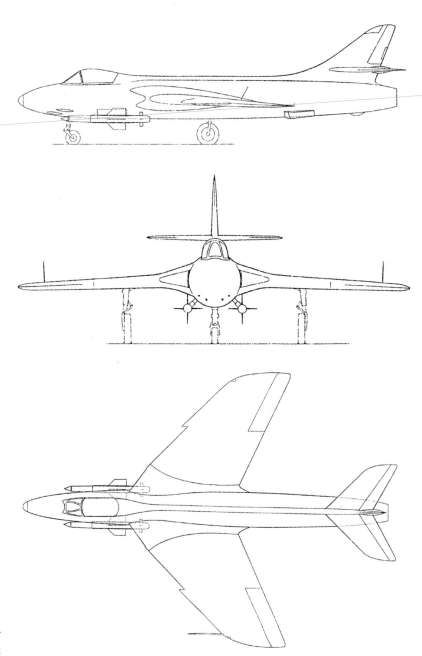

The July 1960 study showing two Firestreaks on a self-contained pack, which replaced the standard Hunter gun pack, the missiles being 'attached' to the sides of the lower forward fuselage.

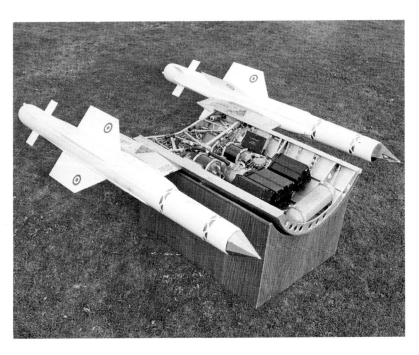

Images of the P.1109B made privately during its Firestreak trials are rare but this shot came from an unknown photographer and was probably taken at Farnborough. Although of poor quality it does show a different angle.

Dummy Firestreak package of the form that was designed in 1960 to fit in the Hunter's forward fuselage.

In July 1960 there was renewed interest from Fighter Command towards improving the air-to-air capability of Hunters based overseas. As a result Hawker and de Havilland proposed a simple conversion allowing two Firestreaks to be carried on a self-contained pack, which replaced the standard Hunter gun pack, the missiles being 'attached' to the sides of the lower forward fuselage. By September, however, it had been decided that two guns were still required together with the missiles and so the idea was dropped.

On 27 June 1957 WW594 went to RAF West Raynham to be used for special trials on the pilot operation of AI radar. After January 1958 the aircraft appears to have been converted back to normal Mk.6 configuration, and two years later it was returned to Hawker Siddeley Aviation (HSA), which Hawker Aircraft at Kingston had now become, for conversion into an FR.Mk.10 tactical fighter reconnaissance aircraft for the RAF. In the mid-1970s it was converted again into an F.Mk.70A for Lebanon.

On 18 August 1957 WW598 flew to Defford, and sometime around early October it also went to West Raynham for service trials. From February 1958

XF378 pictured flying in formation with other Hunters during a Farnborough photo shoot. XF310 with its Fireflash weapons appears just underneath the end fuselage.

A picture of WW598 taken towards the end of its RAE career and now in a different but still attractive blue and white scheme. (Peter Green Collection)

the aircraft was used by the Royal Radar Establishment for trials with the Red Steer radar, and then between April 1959 and 1967 WW598 was on the strength of RAE Bedford, before going to RAE Farnborough on 3 August 1967. Soon after its missile equipment was removed WW598 was used for intensive flight trials to examine the effects of severe gusts on aeroplanes flying at very low altitudes and high speeds and in high temperatures, part of the general research carried out for low level strike aircraft like the Blackburn Buccaneer and BAC TSR.2. During the mid-1960s (and still with the longer nose) it was used regularly by RAE as a chase plane, for example for the BAC.221 high-speed research aircraft, and on 28 May 1968 it went to RAE Llanbedr to serve as a high-altitude shepherd aircraft for target drones. On 7 May 1974 WW598 was repurchased by HSA and converted into a Mk.70A and in 1975 it was delivered to Lebanon. The 'Design Certificate for Flight Trials of Service Aircraft' sheet issued for WW598 on 18 July 1957 gave a normal take-off weight (for all forms of flying) of 17,000lb (7,711kg) and an overload take-off weight (gentle manoeuvres) of 19,250lb (8,732kg). The maximum permitted speed was 620 knots (714mph/1,149km/h) or Mach 1.0 indicated, although Mach 1.16 had been attained during contractor's flight testing, and spinning was prohibited.

After spending time in de Havilland's hands, from 21 October 1957 XF378 was used by A&AEE Boscombe Down for flight trials, and from 2 January 1958 by Hawker for flight load testing. On 5 July 1959 it was sold back to Hawker, although some sources state that XF378 was in fact written off in 1959 after a fuselage fire and cannibalised for spare parts. A memorandum from Air Vice Marshal Satterly, Assistant Chief of the Air Staff (Operational Requirements), dated 19 March 1956, indicated that a second airframe was also to have had the Firestreak/AI.20 radar combination fitted, but added that at this stage it was not yet possible to allocate 'any of the scarce experimental models of AI.20 for these aircraft'. This final airframe conversion was not completed.

In the September 1979 issue of *Air International* magazine test pilot Sqn Ldr R.N. 'Bob' Broad remembered flying the P.1109 at the CFE at West Raynham, where they referred to the aircraft as the 'Hunter night fighter'. He noted that it was 'wildly unsuccessful in its planned role due to the poor radar' and declared that AI.20 was the radar that could not be jammed 'for by no stretch of the imagination could the picture become worse'. However, the P.1109 was 'an outstanding performer at high altitude, easily outclassing a standard Hunter 6'. Broad added that although CFE did not have time to do any proper tests it did fly at less engine rpm and turned tighter. Recently he has corresponded with the author on the subject and has added the following:

You will not be surprised to learn that after fifty-five years or so my memories are not all that reliable – some things I remember clearly – others not at all. I have used my logbook as my main reference for sorties; unfortunately my logbook is often rather curt on what a sortie actually did. First, however, an interesting point was raised through some remarks made by my CO in that there had in the past been what might be called a demarcation dispute as to whether AFDS (the Air Fighting Development Squadron) or AWDS (the All-Weather Development Squadron) should handle the forthcoming aircraft from English Electric that would become the Lightning when it entered service. You can imagine the arguments – AWDS familiar with radar – AFDS the home of the single seat fighter. AFDS won and in due course was awarded the role of looking after the Lightning.

So when the P.1109 appeared on the scene at CFE I was told that its role was to give us pilots experience on a single-seat radar-equipped fighter; in other words we weren't really evaluating the P.1109, we were evaluating us. Actually AFDS, thinking ahead, had recruited a pilot with suitable experience obtained on an exchange tour with the USAF [United States Air Force]. He had I gathered worked with a very similar system to the 1109's AI.20, which the USAF had abandoned, and he briefed me on the basic techniques of flying a pattern to provide a target for the radar, but took little part in the trials himself – he knew it already.

As far as AFDS was concerned the P.1109 was a Hunter 6 and it is recorded as such in my log book; however, it was a Hunter 6 with AI.20 radar. There was some plumbing for Firestreaks which was not evident and the main distinguishing feature was a radar display in the centre of the instrument panel. AI.20 was I think a spiral scan radar and the display was a little peculiar. If the aircraft was pointing straight at the target then a circle was displayed on the screen – the nearer you were to the target the larger the circle. If you were not pointing at the target then an arc would appear on the circle where you weren't pointing, so to get the P.1109 aimed at the target you steered towards the arc in the circle. However, it was very difficult to tell at just what angle off you were flying to the target which then made it very difficult to get into an attacking position. Once lined up at small angles off AI.20 was quite precise and well suited to lining up a missile. If you could close to a target say to a range of within about 3 miles (4.8km) the AI.20 worked well and was very straightforward, but as I say it was not at all easy to get into such a position.

Most of the sorties I have listed for WW594 and WW598 are shown marked as 'Familiarisation' or 'Intercepts' – effectively the same – which were attempts to pick up a target aircraft or 'stooge' and then get into the rear quarter position. As stated this was not easy even under ideal conditions and was probably the reason why the AI.20 concept was not followed up. The system I think made for a very simple radar but was very difficult to operate. The maximum range as far as I can recall was not much more than 10 miles (16.1km) and judging the angle off at that range was very tricky indeed – in fact I did once convert my intercept into an unanticipated head-on attack!! I did, however, begin to get the hang of it and my last radar sortie in WW598 is recorded as 'four successful intercepts', but it must be said that this was at medium altitudes; it was clearly going to be much more difficult to operate at heights of say around 45,000ft (13,716m) where the aircraft was less manoeuvrable.

The list of sorties made by the P.1109s while at CFE show that the intensity of the flying was very low. AFDS did not leave aircraft on the ground deliberately – if an aircraft was serviceable it would be flown either on one of the many trials going on or on continuation training. It would not sit idle. So the implication which agrees with my memory is that the serviceability of the P.1109 was very poor and this can be attributed mostly to the unreliability of the AI.20. The schedule shows WW594 even going back to its home at RRE for presumably some specialist attention.

Apart from playing with the radar the flights with AI.20 running did suggest that the P.1109 was slightly easier on fuel than an accompanying standard Mk.6; however we were not (I think regrettably) interested in evaluating the P.1109's airframe. Nevertheless in late 1957, following the Sandys Defence Review and the cutbacks to Fighter Command, DFLS (Day Fighter Leader School) found it difficult to arrange opposition for their fighter sweeps which came at the end of their course. AFDS were pressed into service to help and it was quite amusing to watch a DFLS formation of Hunter F.Mk.6s, clearly impressively briefed and organised, as they set off, to be followed by a motley formation of whatever AFDS had available. Usually, but not always, we would be outclassed flying Hunter F.Mk.4s or 5s but sometimes we would have a brand new F.Mk.6 with an electric tail and extended leading edge at our disposal. A lot also depended on the calibre of the opposition – one would struggle against a pilot who had done a tour on North American F-86 Sabres in Korea, but on other occasions we would be flying against a potential squadron commander fresh from a tour in the Air Ministry. On the whole we more than held our own whatever we were flying.

On one of those sorties WW594 was available and it was planned that the aircraft would lead the AFDS formation and (we hoped) act as a primitive AEW aircraft, thereby giving us a much-needed edge. I had in fact tried to work out how a formation of eight aircraft would appear on the AI.20's screen. However, when I got to 10,000ft (3,048m) and switched the radar on it failed immediately – among other undesirable features of AI.20 was that it had a massive ground effect and wasn't any use below 10,000ft (3,048m). Undeterred the AFDS formation split up into pairs and went hunting for DFLS who we knew were somewhere over the Thames Estuary. I had a standard Hunter Mk.6 as my Number 2 and we went up to about 50,000ft (15,240m) where he was having the greatest difficulty in keeping up with me while the P.1109 still had plenty in hand. So much so that when it came to the DFLS formation I left him struggling but able to clear my tail while I effortlessly picked off a section of DFLS Hunters, finishing by passing straight between them at quite an overtaking speed. It was an unforgettable demonstration of the aerodynamics of the P.1109.

I understand that the official altitude record for a Hunter was Hugh Merewether in a P.1109 reaching 55,000ft (16,764m), but in fact I was once able to beat this flying from Farnborough in a brand new very light F.Mk.1 with no guns installed. Thanks to the weather conditions being just right I was able to reach an indicated 56,800ft (17,313m) on that particular day, which with calculations for error came out at just about 57,000ft (17,374m).

The P.1109 was a lovely aeroplane but flying it at AFDS was eventually abandoned, due I think to the difficulty in getting any serviceability from the AI.20. The system had served its purpose in giving several single-seat fighter pilots an introduction to radar, but not anything more.

The Hunter P.1109 programme is just one small element of the development process that brought forth new high performance fighters in the 1950s and the first generation of air-to-air guided weapons that came with them. It was an interesting and worthwhile exercise and the P.1109 was regarded by many as the best looking of all Hunters.

Engine and Powerplant Test Beds

On 26 January 1954 Hunter F.Mk.2 WN889 was flown from Baginton to Bitteswell as part of Armstrong Siddeley's Sapphire engine research programme. It then flew with a Sapphire Sa.6 Series 12 giving 8,400lb (37.3kN) of thrust and in August 1955 a Hawker pilot visited Bitteswell to carry out a brief assessment of the installation. The pilot found that the engine handling characteristics were satisfactory in that no surge of malfunction could be induced but the gain in performance from the increased thrust rating was reduced at altitude. WN889 was Struck Off Charge on 10 September 1957 and sent to the Proof & Experimental Establishment (PEE) at Shoeburyness.

The second production F.Mk.5 WN955 was fitted with an Armstrong Siddeley Sapphire Sa.7 series engine to become (in what was termed by *Flight* magazine) a 'Mk.6 standby', presumably against failure of the Avon Mk.6 programme. The Sa.7 was placed in the same category as the Avon RA.24, it could be readily fitted to the Hunter and with 11,000lb (48.9kN) of thrust was expected to give the same performance (although increases in the air intake

Hunter F.Mk.2 WN889 was used as a Sapphire testbed. (Rolls-Royce Heritage Trust)

The thrust reverser Hunter XF833. (Peter Green Collection)

would be necessary). First flown on 26 October 1954, WN955 was handed over to the Ministry of Supply test fleet at Bitteswell in November and in 1955 it was converted to take the more powerful engine, making its first flight with this installed on 9 February 1956 piloted by Armstrong Whitworth's Flt Lt W.H. Bill Else. As such it carried the Class B mark 'G-1-2' and was painted silver. From November 1956 the aircraft was used by A&AEE for banner and sleeve target towing (almost certainly with the standard Sa.6 back in position), and from mid-July 1959 it was used by RAE Farnborough's Radio Department for ground experiments with the engine running for infra-red trials. WN955 was Struck Off Charge on 15 July 1960 and destroyed on the Farnborough fire dump in 1967. Ministry documents show that there was a proposal in June 1956 to uprate the Hunter F.Mks.2 and 5's 8,150lb (36.2kN) thrust Sapphire

Spectacular photo of XF833 with the thrust reverser and smoke generator in operation. (Rolls-Royce Heritage Trust)

Close ups of the thrust reverser installation. (Peter Green Collection)

6s to 8,600lb (38.2kN) Sapphire 12s on overhaul – the Sa.6 became the Sa.12 through modifications to the turbine and a change of material in the first row of turbine blades.

The F.Mk.6 prototype XF833 was used for the flight development programme of the Rolls-Royce thrust reverser under an MoS contract, Hawker being informed in early June 1954 that such an installation was to be done on an F.Mk.6. To this end XF833 was provided with an orifice on each side of the jet pipe in which was mounted a pair of hemispherical eyelid shutters. When reverse thrust was selected these were closed and all of the Avon RA.28 engine efflux was forced to go out through new lateral rectangular outlet grill exits in the sides of the rear fuselage, each of which had multiple cascade vanes positioned such that they would deflect the exhaust outwards and forwards. The conversion, which involved little external modification to engine or airframe, took place in May and June 1956 at Miles Aircraft at Shoreham. XF833 was delivered by road to Rolls-Royce's test airfield at Hucknall in July, and at the September 1956 SBAC Show a smoke generator bottle in the tailpipe was used to show the direction of gas flow (which in fact at times completely immersed the aircraft in smoke). In the cockpit for the show's

XF833 comes in to land at Farnborough in 1956.

demonstration flying was Rolls-Royce's chief test pilot A.J. 'Jim' Heyworth DFC and Bar who had held the position since 1954.

The initial landing tests were performed in November and December 1956 and embraced nearly 130 reversals and, since Hucknall's runway length would not permit no-brake landings, all of the tests were made using full braking plus the reverser. Furthermore, there was a speed limit imposed in that the reverser could not be employed at speeds under 80 knots (92mph/148km/h) because of the control surface flutter created by the forward thrust of the exhaust efflux. It was established that the landing roll distance using full braking without reverse thrust stretched to 2,520ft (768m), while the average figure with the reverser in operation saw the landing roll distance cut by some 919ft (280m). It was also calculated that without any landing restrictions and maintaining the reverse thrust until the aircraft came to a halt might reduce the landing roll by 56 per cent. Altogether 308 landings were accomplished before XF833 went to RAE Bedford in April 1958. The programme's objective was to prove the operation and reliability of the thrust reverser, with its principal applications connected with the Rolls-Royce Conway engine aboard future long-range airliners.

Other Notable Research and Trials Aircraft

F.Mk.1 WT562 was given one-third-span flaps in a trials installation while in 1954 WT568 received a saw-tooth wing leading edge extension at Boscombe Down. F.Mk.4 WT780 was fitted with a Plessey ram-air turbine in its rear fuselage to provide an emergency supply for the elevators and this same aircraft also received a tail hook and was used for drag chute development. Additionally it was tested with a five-camera 'FR' nose as part of a privately funded project leading to the FR.Mk.10 Hunter, before being broken up in November 1964. XF379 was an F.Mk.6 fitted with lateral airbrakes taken from prototype WB188 but which were not taken up. First flown on 20 November 1956 F.Mk.6 XG290 spent the majority of its long flying career on trials work with various establishments and this lasted into the 1980s, including for example trials with revised gun ports.

Farnborough Shows 1956 and 1957

These two SBAC Shows, which both took place in the early Septembers of their respective years, featured a batch of individual Hunter demonstration airframes flying a co-ordinated display as a major highlight of each event. The 1956 show saw performances by the thrust reverser Hunter XF833, Fireflash

carrier XF310, the first two-seat prototype, two F.Mk.6s XG128 and XG129 with a mix of underwing stores and XG131. XG128 carried two 100gal (455lit) asbestos phenolic tanks plus twenty-four 3in (7.62cm) rocket projectiles while XG129 had four of the 100gal (455lit) tanks with the inner pylon under each wing raked forward and outer pylons straight.

XG131 was an entirely new variant of the Hunter, which was described by the manufacturers as an interceptor and ground attack development aircraft for the MoS. It was fitted with 85gal (386lit) part underslung metal tip tanks which were attached permanently over the normal wing tip by a finely and attractively faired sleeve. The tanks had navigation lights and pitot heads mounted in their noses while in other respects XG131 was a normal Mk.6. The aircraft first flew on 16 August 1956 and may have had the tip tanks from the start – it was certainly flying with them by the end of the month when unacceptable buffet was experienced. Hawker test pilot Duncan Simpson told the author that the presence of the faired tip tanks destroyed or wrecked the Hunter's aerodynamics, particularly at high incidence – using underwing tanks was a much better option. After Farnborough (where XG131 appeared only in the static show) Hawker decided not to continue with development of the tip tank installation, and in fact no Ministry support was given to this project. The airframe was subsequently converted back to the normal Mk.6 configuration, being delivered to No.5 Maintenance Unit at Kemble on 10 October 1956. As restored it was supplied to No.14 Squadron in June 1957, and on 19 March 1971 crashed into high ground killing its pilot.

At the 1957 show there was the Fireflash airframe XF310 again, standard F.Mk.6 XK147 which was displayed in the static park with the latest modifications including the dog-tooth wing extension and a yaw-stabiliser (plus a large variety of different weaponry laid around it), and the Firestreak carrier XF378 which, when making high-speed, low-level passes, was seen to produce some quite extraordinary formations of shockwaves. Other Mk.6s at the show were serials XE587 and XK148, which appeared alongside T.Mk.7s XJ615 and XJ627.

XG131 with its faired tip tanks is seen in the static park at Farnborough in September 1956.
The aircraft was mounted on jacks.

Close up of XG131's tip tank fitting. (Phil Butler)

General view of XG131 at Farnborough 1956. The
aircraft is now standing on its own undercarriage.

Group photo of Hunters displayed at the 1956 SBAC Show. XF310 is nearest (top) while
the rest (left to right) are XG128, XG129, XG131 and XJ615.

Air-to-air photograph of F.Mk.6 XK148 armed with no less than thirty-six 3in (7.62cm) rocket projectiles. XK148 attended the 1957 Farnborough Show.

F.Mk.6 XG290 spent most of its flying career on research work.

PROPOSED and PLANNED MODIFICATIONS and DEVELOPMENTS

Hawker Aircraft looked at a number of improved and advanced versions of the basic Hunter airframe, a selection of which are described below. Apart from the plans to produce the P.1083 none of the design proposals were to have been built.

P.1083

RAE Farnborough first recommended producing a research aircraft having 50 degrees of sweep on its wing leading edge on 29 September 1949. In August 1950 the Director of Operational Requirements reported that, although the P.1067 itself was superior to the new Soviet Mikoyan MiG-15 jet fighter, the margin was 'not outstanding'. As a result, and after an approach had been made to Hawker by the Ministry, late in 1950 Sydney Camm's design team put together a preliminary proposal for a P.1067 fitted with a 50 degrees sweep wing. However, at this early stage it was a case of taking the basic airframe and attaching a new set of wings to the existing pick up points, the only fuselage modification being the strengthening of the rear spar frame while the intakes would be unaffected.

On 31 May 1951 an official brochure was submitted for an 'F.3/48 Development Thin Wing Hunter' which had a 50 degrees swept wing instead of the P.1067 Hunter's 35 degrees sweep at the leading edge, and which also had the wing thickness reduced from 8.5 per cent to 7.5 per cent. The armament was two Aden cannon and the powerplant a reheated Sapphire 4 replacing the reheated Avon RA.7. The firm claimed that the substantial

Original manufacturer's model of the P.1083, which today is in the hands of the Brooklands Museum.

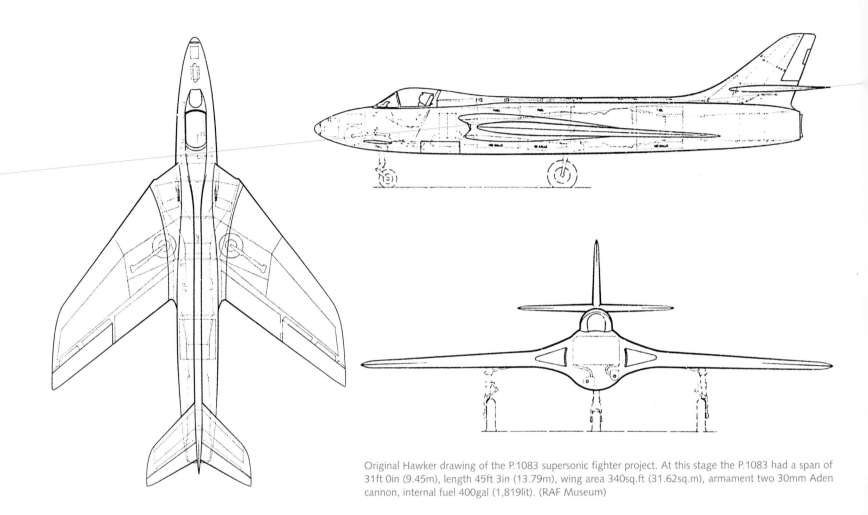

Original Hawker drawing of the P.1083 supersonic fighter project. At this stage the P.1083 had a span of 31ft 0in (9.45m), length 45ft 3in (13.79m), wing area 340sq.ft (31.62sq.m), armament two 30mm Aden cannon, internal fuel 400gal (1,819lit). (RAF Museum)

increase in thrust that the new engine provided, coupled with a reduction in drag, would push the top speed up at all heights by 40mph (64km/h), which would make level speeds in the region of Mach 1.0 possible, while the maximum without the reheat lit was Mach 0.95 to 0.97, an increase of about 30mph (48km/h) on the subsonic P.1067 Hunter. The estimated ceiling would be 53,700ft (16,368m) with reheat, 45,800ft (13,960m) without.

The Ministry realised that the P.1083 had undoubted research value and good potential for military applications, and by now it was also becoming clear that the Hunter itself would not be able to cope with any advanced development of the MiG-15. In addition, although adequate against the current Soviet bomber threat, the British fighter would need the maximum possible performance against a jet bomber threat which (it was thought) might soon arise. By October 1951 plans were sufficiently settled to consider ordering a prototype and an unofficial go-ahead was given on the 17th. At the time it was appreciated that the experimental shop at Hawker was small and so it was not the intention to order a new prototype but rather to adapt the fourth Hunter prototype that was already on order. A full official go-ahead was given by the Ministry on 12 December although the choice of engine for production machines was switched in January 1952 to a 14,500lb (64.4kN) Rolls-Royce RA.14R Avon.

The Hunter could be taken through the 'sound barrier' in a shallow dive but was subsonic on the level. To confer level supersonic speed the P.1083 replaced the Hunter's 35 degrees sweep wing with a new 50 degrees form. Putting models of both types side-by-side (standard Hunter on the left) shows how different the new wing would have appeared.

In June 1952 a meeting was held with the Ministry to discuss the Hunter programme in general, the Air Staff declaring that it was anxious to have the 50 degrees wing and the reheated RA.14 introduced into the Hunter as soon as possible. Hawker reported that the P.1083 prototype should fly in July 1953 but added that the new version needed extra fuel and the design team could not see where this could be provided internally. The meeting finally agreed that the 'thin wing' Hunter development should continue and that its introduction into production was urgent.

Specification F.119D was issued in August 1952 to cover the new design and the prototype was to be powered by an Avon RA.7R. Much of the wing design had been completed by August, work on the wings themselves was started in the Experimental Shop in October, 65 per cent of the drawings had been completed by December 1952 and the aircraft was at this stage forecast to fly in autumn 1953. On 17 February 1953 a mock-up RA.14 engine was assembled into the P.1083 mock-up. However, in early April, and with the prototype well advanced, the Air Staff stated that the P.1083 should now have the de Havilland Blue Jay (Firestreak) air-to-air missile as its primary weapon, but for Hawker the P.1083 had been developed purely as an improved Hunter with guns only and it was not intended to be a guided weapon carrier. The firm was told officially that the Air Staff was now only interested if the aircraft could carry four Blue Jays, but investigations indicated that with these missiles, its guns and 420gal (1,909lit) of internal fuel the P.1083 would be short on cruising endurance. The fighter would also lose manoeuvrability with the missiles aboard and a full redesign would be the only solution.

On 13 July 1953 Hawker was informed officially that the P.1083 was to be cancelled and work would cease forthwith. However, the front and centre fuselage and the tail from the cancelled prototype (which had been given the serial WN470) were in due course used to construct the P.1099 Hunter F.Mk.6 prototype XF833. A Ministry report dated 7 March 1955 notes that by May 1953 the Air Staff had become very concerned at the lack of progress being made in curing the numerous troubles experienced on the original Hunter, which mainly concerned the introduction of reheat, the development of satisfactory airbrakes and the inability to provide more fuel. This unsatisfactory state of affairs on the existing Hunter was an indication of the difficulties which confronted the P.1083 Thin Wing Hunter development, quite apart from the aerodynamic changes involved in fitting a larger engine (also reheated) and the complication attendant on the addition of guided missiles. Therefore, it seemed clear that the P.1083 must be virtually a new aircraft and was unlikely to be available to the RAF within two years after the first Hunter, as originally planned. The estimated development cost had also gone up and so the Ministry, in view of these problems and the need to leave Hawker free to concentrate on the Hunter F.Mk.1's difficulties, decided that the P.1083 should be cancelled in favour of a development of the rival Supermarine Swift fighter called the Type 545 (and which itself was later cancelled).

As a final parting shot, on 23 September 1953 Hawker submitted an updated brochure for a refined P.1083 powered now by a Rolls-Royce RA.19R. The 12,500lb (55.6kN) RA.19 development of the RA.14 with full reheat required no further work for its installation and the reheat was of the infinitely variable type, i.e. any degree of thrust could be used between non-reheat and full reheat. The fuel capacity was now 600gal (2,728lit), which was achieved by introducing the integral wing type tanks then being developed for the Hunter and by increasing the capacity in the rear fuselage. The rear fuselage itself, which would be an integral part of the reheat jet pipe, also had to be redesigned on account of the appreciably larger pipe. The principle here was that the nozzle and outer skin of the jet pipe would in fact be the fuselage, with the jet pipe consisting only of the inner heat-resisting skin.

Aerodynamically it was proposed to modify the wing further by extending the leading edge forward progressively towards the tips, so as to produce a thinner aerofoil section with some degree of camber and washout. The sweepback would be slightly reduced, but the overall result would be an improvement over the original Hunter wing (the construction of the original P.1083 wing had not advanced very far and the brochure added that little will have been lost by its re-design).

The brochure data with the RA.19R engine and 1,800°K of reheat now gave an all-up-weight for the P.1083 with 600gal (2,728lit) of fuel of 20,000lb (9,072kg). Half-fuel weight was 17,700lb (8,029kg) and at this weight the maximum speed at sea level was estimated to be 820mph (1,319km/h) Mach 1.08, at 36,000ft (10,973m) 790mph (1,271km/h) Mach 1.20, and at 55,000ft (16,764m) 690mph (1,110km/h) Mach 1.045. Rate of climb at sea level would be 50,000ft/min (15,240m/min), service ceiling (rate of climb 1,000ft/min/305m/min) 59,500ft (18,136m) and time to 55,000ft (16,764m) 4.62 minutes.

P.1090

This sleek supersonic development of the Hunter had a 50 degrees sweep wing and was to be powered by one reheated de Havilland Gyron turbojet. The project was dated 8 August 1951 and was to have been armed with four 30mm Aden cannon. Its span was 35ft 4in (10.77m), length 51ft 9in (15.77m), wing area 358sq.ft (33.29sq.m) and fuel capacity 400gal (1,819lit).

P.1091

A subsonic Hunter derivative was the P.1091 project dated 12 October 1951, which was given a delta wing with 60 degrees of sweep on the leading edge, one reheated 8,000lb (35.6kN) Armstrong Siddeley Sapphire 4 and four 30mm Aden cannon. The maximum speed was given as Mach 0.98 and the study was undertaken along with Avro, one assumes to make use of that company's experience in designing delta wing aeroplanes such as the Vulcan bomber and the 707 scale model research aircraft associated with it. The P.1091's span was 33ft 0in (10.06m), overall length 41ft 11in (12.78m) and wing area 510sq.ft (47.43sq.m); the fuel capacity was 420gal (1,910lit).

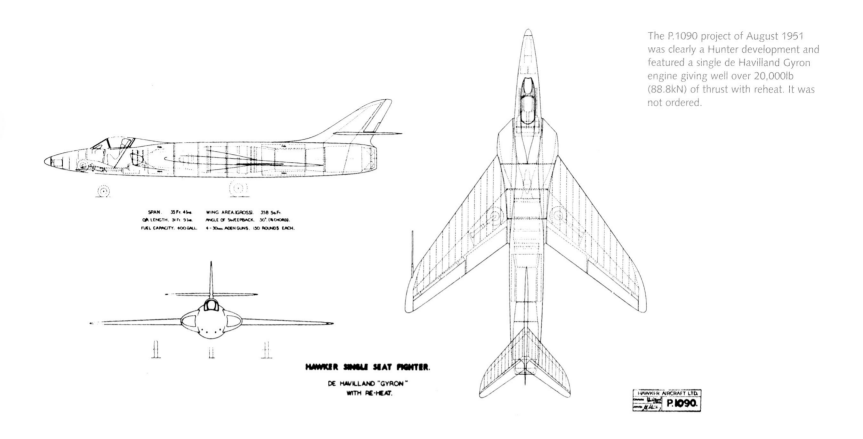

The P.1090 project of August 1951 was clearly a Hunter development and featured a single de Havilland Gyron engine giving well over 20,000lb (88.8kN) of thrust with reheat. It was not ordered.

SPAN. 35 Ft. 4 Ins.   WING AREA. (GROSS). 358 Sq.Ft.
OA LENGTH. 51 Ft. 9 Ins. ANGLE OF SWEEPBACK. 50° (¼ CHORD).
FUEL CAPACITY. 400 GALL. 4 - 30mm. ADEN GUNS. 150 ROUNDS EACH.

HAWKER SINGLE SEAT FIGHTER.

DE HAVILLAND "GYRON"
WITH RE-HEAT.

HAWKER AIRCRAFT LTD.
P.1090.

Model of the Hawker P.1090 made by Joe Cherrie.

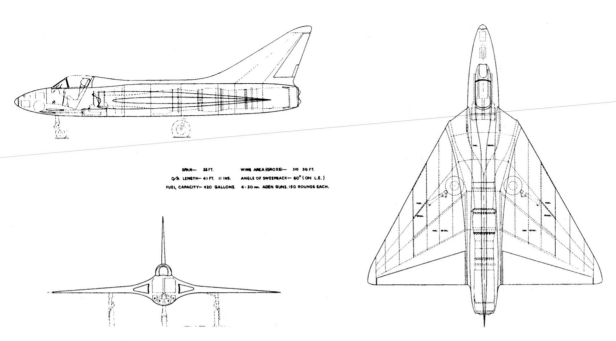

The Hawker P.1091 delta wing project. Despite the different wing clearly this design was still part of the Hunter family.

SPAN— 33 FT.   WING AREA (GROSS)— 510 SQ. FT.
O/A LENGTH— 41 FT. II INS.   ANGLE OF SWEEPBACK— 60° (ON L.E.)
FUEL CAPACITY— 420 GALLONS.   4 - 30 m. ADEN GUNS. 150 ROUNDS EACH.

HAWKER SINGLE SEAT FIGHTER.
F3/48 WITH DELTA WINGS.
ARMSTRONG SIDDELEY "SAPPHIRE 4."
WITH RE-HEAT.

HAWKER AIRCRAFT LIMITED.
P. 1091.

Beautifully detailed model of the P.1091 made by Joe Cherrie.

P.1100

Another Hawker study for a Hunter variant to carry the Blue Jay/Firestreak missile was the supersonic 'thin wing' P.1100 project of mid-1953. This was intended to carry two Aden cannon, two missiles and the AI.20 radar and would be powered by an RA.24 Avon. It would also have a rocket motor in each trailing edge wing root and was expected to achieve Mach 1.5. Span 35ft 6in (10.82m), length 52ft 0in (15.85m), gross wing area 343sq.ft (31.90sq.m), internal fuel 680gal (3,092lit).

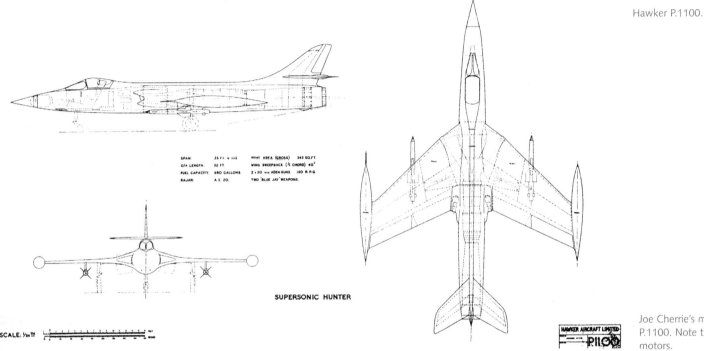

Hawker P.1100.

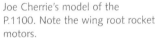

Joe Cherrie's model of the P.1100. Note the wing root rocket motors.

P.1102

This Hunter development of 27 October 1953 used a reheated Avon RA.19R and had the main undercarriage housed in extended wing root fairings. Just the two 30mm Aden cannon were housed in the lower nose and the wing had 45 degrees of sweep at the quarter chord line. Span 34ft 4in (10.46m), overall length 47ft 5in (14.45m), wing area 368sq.ft (34.22sq.m).

P.1105

A 1954 proposal for a standard Hunter F.Mk.6 fitted with a podded Napier TRR/37 rocket engine under each wing and an Avon RA.23 jet. The fuel capacities were 330gal (1,500lit) for the Avon and 60gal (273lit) for the rocket, along with another 310gal (1,410lit) of oxidant.

Hawker P.1102.

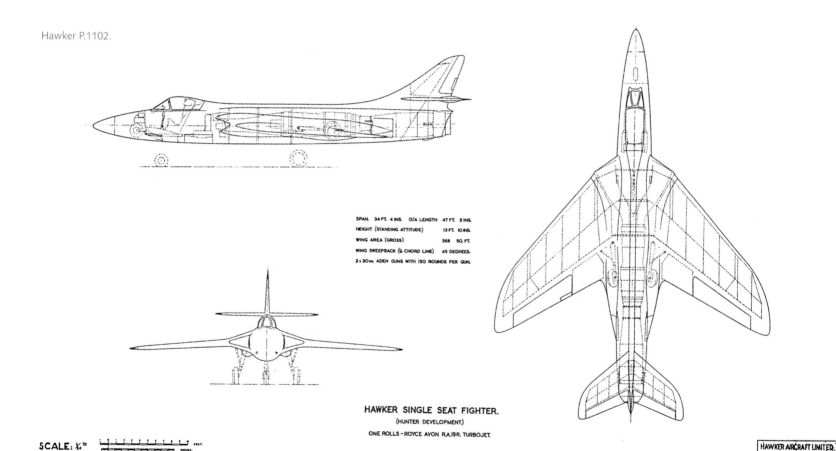

SPAN. 34 FT. 4 INS. O/A LENGTH 47 FT. 5 INS.
HEIGHT (STANDING ATTITUDE) 13 FT. 10 INS.
WING AREA (GROSS) 368 SQ.FT.
WING SWEEPBACK (¼ CHORD LINE) 45 DEGREES.
2 x 30 mm ADEN GUNS WITH 150 ROUNDS PER GUN.

HAWKER SINGLE SEAT FIGHTER.
(HUNTER DEVELOPMENT.)
ONE ROLLS - ROYCE AVON R.A.19R. TURBOJET.

SCALE: ¼ TH FEET. INCHES.

HAWKER AIRCRAFT LIMITED.
P.1102

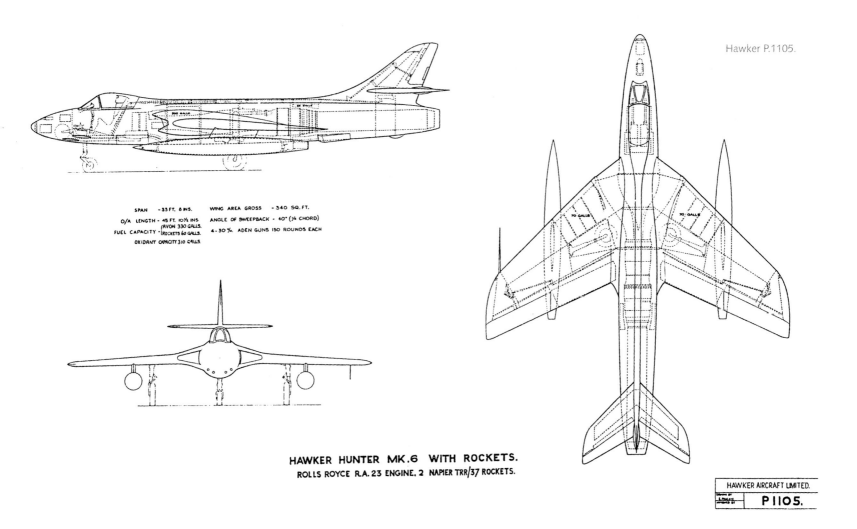

SPAN   -33 FT. 8 INS.
O/A LENGTH - 45 FT. 10¾ INS
(AVON 330 GALLS.
FUEL CAPACITY - ROCKETS 60 GALLS.
OXIDANT CAPACITY 310 GALLS.

WING AREA GROSS   - 340 SQ. FT.
ANGLE OF SWEEPBACK - 40° (¼ CHORD)
4 - 30 %. ADEN GUNS 150 ROUNDS EACH

HAWKER HUNTER MK.6 WITH ROCKETS.
ROLLS ROYCE R.A. 23 ENGINE. 2 NAPIER TRR/37 ROCKETS.

Hawker P.1105.

HAWKER AIRCRAFT LIMITED.
P 1105.

P.1106

This Hunter project had a large span 40 degrees sweep thin wing of 6 per cent t/c ratio, an Armstrong Siddeley Sapphire Sa.10 engine, AI.20 radar and two underwing Blue Jay (Firestreak) missiles; there were no guns. Date 5 October 1954. Span 38ft 0in (11.58m), length 48ft 1in (14.65m), wing area 362sq.ft (33.67sq.m).

P.1117

A twin Firestreak-armed Hunter development of 1955, prepared for the Royal Navy, which had fixed wing tip fuel tanks, an Avon RA.24 engine, AI.23 radar and two Aden guns. Span 35ft 4in (10.77m), length 49ft 4in (15.04m), fuel capacity 340gal (1,546lit).

Hawker P.1106.

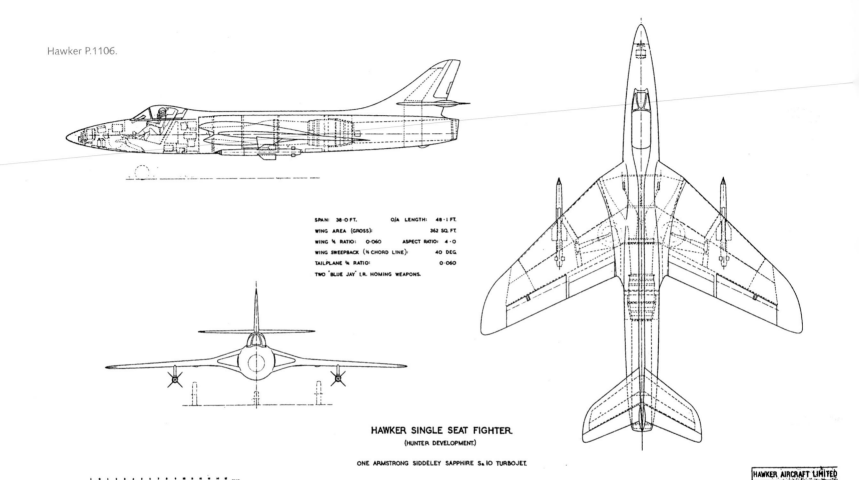

SPAN: 38·0 FT.   O/A LENGTH: 48·1 FT.

WING AREA (GROSS):   362 SQ. FT.

WING ¼ RATIO: 0·060   ASPECT RATIO: 4·0

WING SWEEPBACK (¼ CHORD LINE):   40 DEG.

TAILPLANE ¼ RATIO: 0·060

TWO 'BLUE JAY' I.R. HOMING WEAPONS.

HAWKER SINGLE SEAT FIGHTER.
(HUNTER DEVELOPMENT.)

ONE ARMSTRONG SIDDELEY SAPPHIRE S₄ 10 TURBOJET.

SCALE: ¹⁄₄ᵗ ᵗ

HAWKER AIRCRAFT LIMITED

P.1106.

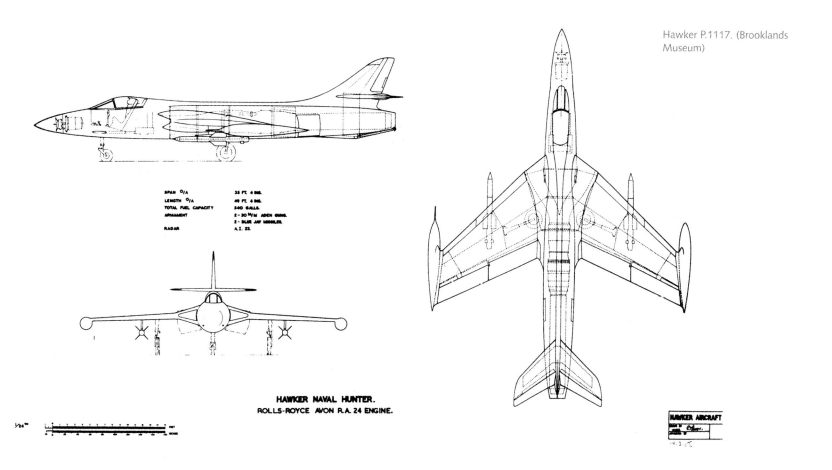

Hawker P.1117. (Brooklands Museum)

SPAN O/A	35 FT. 4 INS.
LENGTH O/A	49 FT. 4 INS.
TOTAL FUEL CAPACITY	540 GALLS.
ARMAMENT	2 - 30 M/M ADEN GUNS.
	2 - BLUE JAY MISSILES.
RADAR	A.I. 23.

HAWKER NAVAL HUNTER.
ROLLS-ROYCE AVON R.A. 24 ENGINE.

HAWKER AIRCRAFT

Joe Cherrie model of the Hawker P.1117 with fixed tip tanks and underwing missiles.

P.1133

This was a proposed all-weather fighter version of the F.Mk.6 Hunter with an AI.23 radar in a long nose, Avon Mk.203 turbojet, two Firestreaks and two Aden cannon; date 1 August 1958. The wing had 40 degrees of sweep at quarter chord. Span 33ft 8in (10.26m), length 49ft 1in (14.96m), wing area 349sq.ft (32.46sq.m), fuel 390gal (1,773lit).

P.1135

Another thin-wing Hunter development but here with a Rolls-Royce RB.146 engine giving 13,200lb (58.7kN) of thrust dry and 18,300lb (81.3kN) with 2,000°K reheat, 16 January 1959. This also had larger wing root intakes to supply the greater quantity of air required by the more powerful engine, an AI.23 Airpass fire control system and four 30mm Aden cannon. Fairey Fireflash missiles were listed as an alternative armament. Overall length 52ft 0in (15.85m), all-up-weight (clean) 21,000lb (9,526kg), internal fuel 550gal (2,501lit), external fuel 400gal (1,819lit) or 660gal (3,001lit).

Hawker P.1133. (Brooklands Museum)

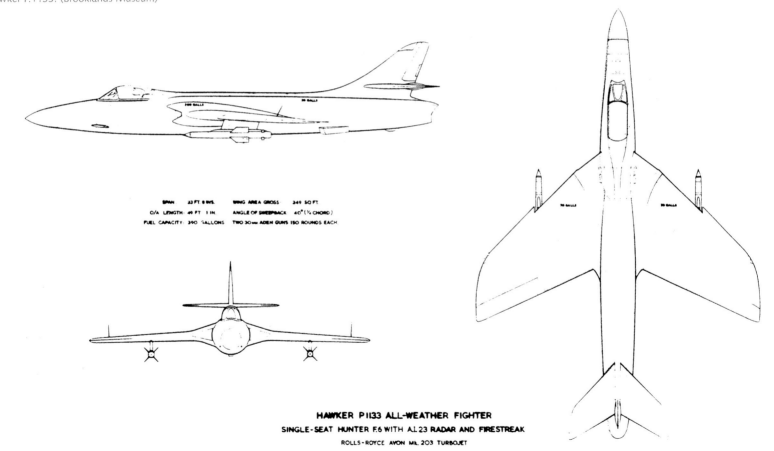

HAWKER P 1133 ALL-WEATHER FIGHTER
SINGLE-SEAT HUNTER F.6 WITH AI.23 RADAR AND FIRESTREAK
ROLLS-ROYCE AVON MK. 203 TURBOJET

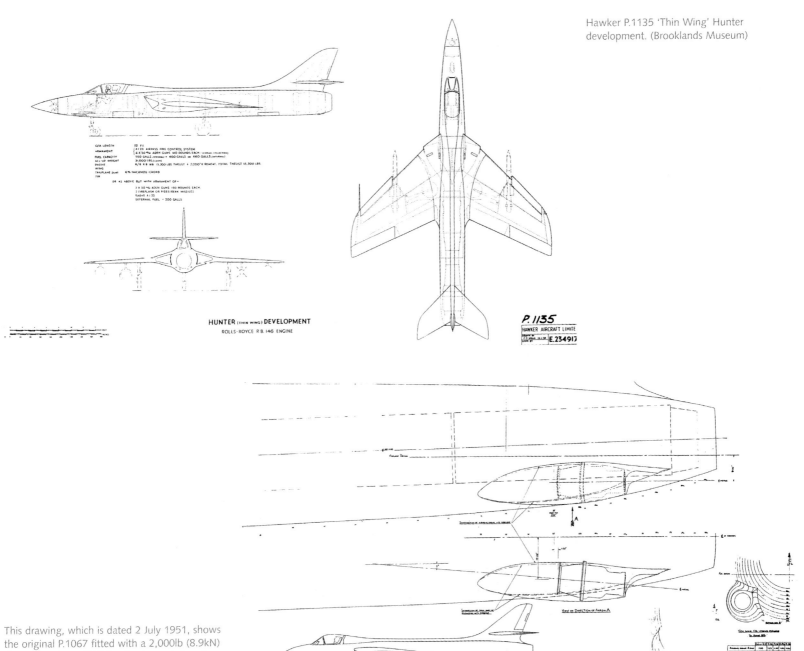

Hawker P.1135 'Thin Wing' Hunter
development. (Brooklands Museum)

HUNTER (THIN WING) DEVELOPMENT
ROLLS-ROYCE R.B. 146 ENGINE

P.1135
HAWKER AIRCRAFT LIMITED
E.234917

This drawing, which is dated 2 July 1951, shows
the original P.1067 fitted with a 2,000lb (8.9kN)
thrust Armstrong Siddeley Snarler rocket motor
on each side of the end fuselage in special
fairings. The rocket motor fuel was to be carried
externally in two 210gal (955lit) underwing
drop tanks. (Brooklands Museum)

HAWKER HUNTER DATA

Note: Pure fighter and trainer versions in long term production only – updates and modified versions are omitted. Information varies with different sources and often reflects different flying conditions. The figures were mostly taken from manufacturer's, Ministry and A&AEE documents. Data for clean condition unless stated, with clean all-up-weight from 1957 A&AEE report based on full internal fuel, full ammunition but no external stores.

F.Mk.1

Span: 33ft 8in (10.26m), length: 45ft 10.5in (13.98m), wing area: 340sq.ft (31.62sq.m)
All-up-weight: 16,200lb (7,348kg)
Internal fuel: 330gal (1,500lit)
Powerplant: 1 x 7,550lb (33.6kN) thrust Rolls-Royce Avon RA.7
Maximum speed: 608 knots (700mph/1,126km/h) at sea level, 524 knots (603mph/970km/h) at 45,000ft (13,716m)
Maximum speed in a dive: Mach 1.2
Ceiling (1,000ft/min/305m/min climb rate): 46,100ft (14,051m)
Ceiling (100ft/min/30m/min climb rate): 50,000ft (15,240m)
Armament: 4 x 30mm Aden cannon

F.Mk.2

Span: 33ft 8in (10.26m), length: 45ft 10.5in (13.98m), wing area: 340sq.ft (31.62sq.m)
All-up-weight: 16,300lb (7,394kg)
Internal fuel: 310gal (1,410lit)

Powerplant: 1 x 8,000lb (35.6kN) thrust Armstrong Siddeley Sapphire Sa.6 Mk.101
Maximum speed: 529 knots (609mph/980km/h) at 45,000ft (13,716m)
Maximum speed in a dive: Mach 1.2
Ceiling (1,000ft/min/305m/min climb rate): 48,300ft (14,722m)
Ceiling (100ft/min/30m/min climb rate): 51,000ft (15,545m)
Armament: 4 x 30mm Aden cannon

F.Mk.4

Span: 33ft 8in (10.26m), length: 45ft 10.5in (13.98m), wing area: 340sq.ft (31.62sq.m)
All-up-weight: 17,100lb (7,757kg)
Maximum gross weight (long range ground attack role with two 1,000lb [454kg] bombs and two 97gal [441lit] drop tanks): 21,200lb (9,616kg)
Internal fuel: 410gal (1,864lit)
Normal maximum fuel with four 97gal (441lit) drop tanks: 798gal (3,628lit)
Powerplant: 1 x 8,050lb (35.8kN) thrust Rolls-Royce Avon RA.21 Mk.113 or 115
Maximum speed (clean, half fuel): 610 knots (702mph/1,130km/h) Mach 0.925 at sea level, 533 knots (614mph/988km/h) Mach 0.93 at 40,000ft (12,192m), 521knots (600mph/965km/h) at 45,000ft (13,716m) (another source says 525 knots (605mph/973km/h) Mach 0.915 at 45,000ft (13,716m))
Maximum speed in a dive: Mach 1.2
Ceiling (1,000ft/min/305m/min climb rate): 45,000ft (13,716m)
Ceiling (100ft/min/30m/min climb rate): 50,000ft (15,240m)
Armament: 4 x 30mm Aden + underwing stores or drop tanks on 2 (later 4) pylons

F.Mk.5

Span: 33ft 8in (10.26m), length: 45ft 10.5in (13.98m), wing area: 340sq.ft (31.62sq.m)
All-up-weight: 17,000lb (7,711kg)
Internal fuel: 392gal (1,782lit)
Powerplant: 1 x 8,000lb (35.6kN) thrust Armstrong Siddeley Sapphire Mk.101
Maximum speed: 612 knots (705mph/1,134km/h) at sea level, 527 knots (607mph/977km/h) at 45,000ft (13,716m)
Maximum speed in a dive: Mach 1.2
Ceiling (1,000ft/min/305m/min climb rate): 47,300ft (14,417m)
Ceiling (100ft/min/30m/min climb rate): 51,000ft (15,545m)
Armament: 4 x 30mm Aden cannon + underwing stores or drop tanks on 2 pylons

F.Mk.6

Span: 33ft 8in (10.26m), length: 45ft 10.5in (13.98m), wing area (with leading edge extensions): 349sq.ft (32.46sq.m)

All-up-weight: 17,800lb (8,074kg)

Maximum take-off weight (maximum external fuel + stores): 23,800lb (10,796kg)

Internal fuel: 392gal (1,782lit)

External fuel: 4 x 100gal (454lit) drop tanks or 2 x 100gal (454lit) + 2 x 230gal (1,046lit) drop tanks

Powerplant: 1 x 10,000lb (44.4kN) thrust Rolls-Royce Avon RA.28 Mk.207

Maximum speed: 621 knots (715mph/1,150km/h) at sea level, 541 knots (623mph/1,002km/h) Mach 0.945 at 36,000ft (10,973m), 535 knots (616mph/991km/h) at 45,000ft (13,716m)

Maximum speed in a dive: Mach 1.23

Ceiling (1,000ft/min/305m/min climb rate): 48,500ft (14,783m)

Ceiling (100ft/min/30m/min climb rate): 52,000ft (15,850m)

Turn distance: At 45,000ft (13,716m) when height and speed constant 4nm (7.4km), otherwise 2nm (3.7km)

Armament: 2 x 30mm Aden cannon + underwing bombs (two 500lb/227kg or 1,000lb/454kg), 24 x 3in (7.62mm) rocket projectiles or 4 drop tanks on 4 pylons

T.Mk.7

Span: 33ft 8in (10.26m), length: 45ft 10.5in (13.98m), wing area (with leading edge extensions): 349sq.ft (32.46sq.m)

Loaded weight: 17,200lb (7,802kg)

Overload weight (four 100gal/454lit tanks): 21,200lb (9,616kg)

Internal fuel: 410gal (1,864lit)

External fuel: 4 x 100gal (454lit) drop tanks

Powerplant: 1 Rolls-Royce Avon Mk.113, 115, 119, 120, 121 or 122 (Avon RA.21 Mk.122 rating = 7,775lb [34.6kN])

Maximum speed: 610 knots (702mph/1,130km/h) at sea level

Maximum speed in a dive: Mach 1.20

Absolute ceiling: 49,000ft (14,935m)

Armament: 1 x 30mm Aden under starboard nose + underwing stores or drop tanks

INDEX

INDEX OF PEOPLE

Other titles published by The History Press

The Hunter Story

MARTIN W. BOWMAN

One of the world's greatest aircraft, for three decades pilots enthused about the Hunter and its smooth lines, Rolls-Royce Avon engine, outstanding handling characteristics and lively performance. Designed by Sir Sydney Camm, the genius behind the Hurricane, work on the Hunter commenced late in 1948, but the post-war economic situation in Britain delayed its first flight until 20 July 1951. In September 1953 Neville Duke piloted a Hunter to shatter the world speed record. This book traces the history of the Hunter across RAF and worldwide service, from design and development to the glory days and the unforgettable aerobatic displays with the Black Knights, Black Arrows and Blue Diamonds. A real pilot's aeroplane, the Hunter reigned supreme for fifty years, with the last example retired in July 2001.

978 0 7524 5082 7

The Harrier Story

PETER R. MARCH

he 'Jump-jet' was the world's first vertical/short take-off and landing operational jet aircraft (VSTOL). Developed using the revolutionary Pegasus engine, the Harrier has served the RAF and US Marine Corps for well over 30 years. Here, vividly told, is the fascinating story from tentative hovering by the Hawker P1127 in 1960 to today's frontline Harrier GR9 and AV-8B warplanes. A naval version, the Sea Harrier, entered service with the Royal Navy in 1979. Alongside the RAF Harrier it saw action in the Falklands War in 1982. More recently, Harriers have seen combat over Kosovo, Bosnia and Iraq. In the USA, a license-built version (the AV8-A/B) equips the US Marine Corps and is in service today in Iraq. Harriers also equip air forces in Spain and Thailand.

978 0 7509 4487 8

Tornado ADV: The Last Cold War Interceptor

PETER FOSTER

Originally designed to intercept Soviet bombers striking from the east, the Panavia Tornado Air Defence Variant was conceived as a stop gap, deriving from the hugely successful bomber type. It suffered in its early years from lack of agility and poor systems. However, the advent of more sophisticated missiles and on-board systems gave it the option of when and how to fight and turned this one-time lame duck into a high-value asset, capable of holding its own in the fast-moving air superiority environment. Featuring complete histories of all stations and squadrons to operate this type of aircraft alongside individual airframe histories, and stunningly illustrated with a number of striking colour photographs, this book charts the lifetime of a special aircraft, forming a perfect tribute to the Tornado ADV.

978 0 7524 5936 3

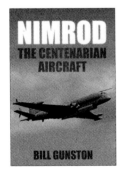

Nimrod The Centenarian Aircraft

BILL GUNSTON

for the first time, this book traces the complete history of the world's first jet airliner, and how this aircraft was developed from the civil airliner the Comet into a sucession of military aircraft named Nimrod, which have been the RAF's primary Marine Patrol Aircraft since the 1970s. Highly respected aviation expert Bill Gunston presents previously unpublished data on unknown Nimrod versions, cutaway drawings and detailed numerical data in the first publication to record dangerous problems with this vitally important RAF aircraft.

978 0 7524 5270 8

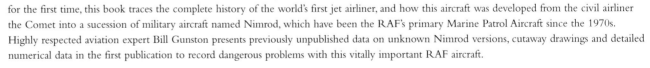

Visit our website and discover thousands of other History Press books.

www.thehistorypress.co.uk